THE

PUBLICATIONS

OF THE

SURTEES SOCIETY

VOL. CLXXXI

THE

PUBLICATIONS

OF THE

SURTEES SOCIETY

ESTABLISHED IN THE YEAR

M.DCCC.XXXIV

VOL. CLXXXI

FOR THE YEAR M.CM.LXVI

At a COUNCIL MEETING of the SURTEES SOCIETY held in Durham Castle on June 16th 1969, Mr. C. R. Hudleston in the chair, it was ORDERED "that Mr. D. J. Rowe's edition of The Records of the Shipwrights' Company of Newcastle upon Tyne should be printed as two volumes of the Society's publications."

W. A. L. SEAMAN
Secretary

THE RECORDS OF THE
COMPANY OF
SHIPWRIGHTS

of

NEWCASTLE UPON TYNE

1622 - 1967

VOLUME II

EDITED BY

D. J. ROWE

PRINTED FOR THE SOCIETY BY
NORTHUMBERLAND PRESS LIMITED
GATESHEAD
1971

CONTENTS

CONTENTS

APPENDIX I

MEMBERS OF THE SHIPWRIGHTS COMPANY

(A) Persons entering the Company by apprenticeship

Date of indenture	Name of apprentice	Christian name of Father	Occupation of Father	Place of origin	Shipwright to whom apprenticed	Date of freedom	Price for freedom
3.6.1616	Edwin Parke	John	Yeoman	Northumberland	Richard Watson		
1.5.1617	Robert Collingwood	George	Gent	Northumberland	Edward Anderson		
1.5.1617	Ralph Totherick	William	Plater	Newcastle	Robert Totherick		
2.2.1618	Robert Browne	Andrew	Yeoman	Northumberland	Richard Readhead		
20.12.1618	Allexander Joplin	John	Yeoman	Mickley[1]	William Carnaby		
14.11.1619	George Taylor	Thomas	Yeoman	Northumberland	Robert Cooke		
29.11.1619	Thomas Crosbie	John	Yeoman	Durham	William Dilahair		
18.4.1620	Roger Muschamp	Roger	Gent	Northumberland	Richard Watson		
2.2.1620	Edward Williamson	Thomas	Shipwright	Newcastle	Richard Readhead		
29.4.1621	John Cowill	Dennis	Yeoman	Cockle Park	Richard Watson		
(6)[2]	William Bamsbie [Gamsbie]				Thomas Colyer		
(8)	Thomas Broune				William Reisley		
(10)	Robert Burton				Robert Watson		
(11)	William Burrell				Robert Totherick		
(17)	Ralph Bowrey				Leonard Bowrey		
(19)	Edward Bullock				Richard Bulman		
(21)	James Blackbeard				Peter Wilkinson		
(4)	Robert Crane				George Johnson		
(4)	Robert Chambers				Edward Draver		
(8)	Christopher Cowen				William Reisley		

205

[1] Where no county is given, the place of origin is in Northumberland, except in the case of such towns as Gateshead and Sunderland, where it was felt unnecessary to suffix Durham.
[2] Folios 3–22 of the volume of indentures are missing and the numbers in brackets refer to the folio number on which the entry was written as given in the index. The index lacks entries for the letter A.

Date of indenture	Name of apprentice	Christian name of Father	Occupation of Father	Place of origin	Shipwright to whom apprenticed	Date of freedom	Price for freedom
(9)	John Carr				George Thompson		
(11)	George Cooke				Mark Cooke		
(11)	James Colthird				Christopher Newton		
(11)	Christopher Crosbie				Thomas Steele		
(15)	William Cooke				Mark Cooke		
(15)	Leonard Coulson				Henry Brantingham		
(15)	Tho. Cooke				Peter Wilkinson		
(17)	William Cooke				Rowl. Steell jun.		
(18)	Hen. Cooke				Tho. Steele		
(18)	Edwin Comin				John Colyer		
(20)	Tho. Cork				Tho. Ogle		
(20)	William Carr				John Carr		
(21)	Andrew Craw				Tho. Steell		
(7)	John Dunn				Robt. Johnson		
(10)	Geo. Dodgshon				Robt Crane		
(20)	John Dixon				William Reasley		
(18)	John Evins				Richard Evins jun.		
(6)	Rowl. Farrow				Edward Anderson		
(9)	Tho. Farrow				Robt Crane		
(12)	Andr. Forster				Thomas Steell		
(19)	William Frissell				Ralph Pattison		
(3)	John Gallen				Peter Wilkinson		
(4)	Robt Gibson				Rowland Steell		
(6)	Will. Gamsbey				Tho. Colyer		
(12)	Edward Green				Geo. Johnson		
(14)	Will. Greenway				Tho. Soulbey		
(17)	Will. Gibson				Tho. Steell		
(19)	Will. Grey				Ralph Pattison		

Date of indenture	Name of apprentice	Christian name of Father	Occupation of Father	Place of origin	Shipwright to whom apprenticed	Date of freedom	Price for freedom
(22)	Robt Grey				Richard Evary		
(4)	John Hodgson				Thomas Steell		
(5)	Roger Hudson				Thomas Steell		
(13)	Will. Harrison				Tho. Whaley		
(18)	Edw. Hall				John Colyer		
(21)	John Hall				William Palmer		
(21)	Roger Harbottle				Peter Wilkinson		
(11)	Geo. Jopling				John Jopling		
(13)	Ra. Jopling				Thomas Catcheside		
(17)	Lance Jopling				Richard Evins		
(10)	William Kell				Edw. Anderson		
(4)	Roger Lumley				Rowland Steell		
(22)	William Lawson				Tho. Whaly		
(5)	Robt Mills				Chr. Knoks		
(6)	Robt Mould				Ralph Davison		
(9)	John Mould				John Hodgson		
(10)	Phillipp Miles				George Thompson		
(16)	Tho. Maxfield				Robert Crane		
(18)	Richard Midleton				William Reasley		
(21)	Math. Maddison				Peter Wilkinson		
(22)	Mich. Moody				Robt Watson		
(3)	Chri. Newton				Rowl. Steell		
(6)	Lionel Nicholson				Tho. Colyer		
(20)	Robert Newton				Geo. Jopling		
(5)	Tho. Ogle				Edward Draver		
(13)	William Ogle				Robt Cooke		
(22)	Tho. Otway				Robt Wailes		
(7)	Cuthbt Poyd				Thomas Colyer		

Date of indenture	Name of apprentice	Christian name of Father	Occupation of Father	Place of origin	Shipwright to whom apprenticed	Date of freedom	Price for freedom
(9)	Tho. Pryor				Peter Hodgshon		
(9)	Willus Palmer				Robt Wailes		
(17)	Rowland Pithie				Robt Steell		
(19)	John Procter				Thom. Whaley		
(22)	Henry Pattison				Robt Watson		
(7)	Edw. Ramsey				William White		
(15)	Geo. Robson				Hen. Brantingham		
(17)	James Reavely				Tho. Steell		
(18)	Tho. Reynick				Timothie Rand		
(20)	John Reay				William Reasley		
(22)	Gawin Robinson				Will. Stevenson		
(22)	Geo. Rand				Geo. Thompson		
(22)	Alex. Rowill				Geo. Thompson		
(5)	Robt Steell				Thomas Steell		
(6)	Anthony Snawdon				Robt Bittleston		
(7)	Tho. Shaftoe				Marke Cooke		
(15)	Edw. Selbie				Robt Cooke		
(20)	John Shevill				William Burrell		
(20)	Rich. Trewhitt				Tho. Mills		
(4)	Edward Uworth				Rowland Steell		
(3)	Edward Wade				Thomas Wade		
(3)	Math. Wilkinson				Robt Totherick		
(7)	Edward Wade				Tho. Wade		
(8)	John Wrangham				Ro. Totherick		
(14)	John Wilkinson				Tho. Soulbey		
(14)	Geo. Will				Marke Cooke		
(19)	John Walker				Leond Coulson		
(20)	Phill. Wilkinson				Edward Green		

Date of indenture	Name of apprentice	Christian name of Father	Occupation of Father	Place of origin	Shipwright to whom apprenticed	Date of freedom	Price for freedom
(21)							
2.2.1630	James Watson				Edward Arrowsmith		
1.8.1630	Robt Champley				Chr. Newton		
30.1.1629	William Read				Christopher Newton		
1.3.1632	Edward White				Roger Peirite		
25.6.1632	John Errington				Roger Perite		
4.6.1632	Thomas Blunt				Rowland Seamer		
10.6.1632	Henry Begg				Rowland Seamer		
2.8.1633	Ralph Swinhoe				John Frizell		
29.9.1634	Robert Davison				John Frizell		
5.11.1633	Heug Colyer				James Colyer		
16.4.1634	Tho. Cuthbert				Richard Evins jun.		
7.5.1634	George Davison				Robt Steell		
11.3.1632	Valentine Marlay				Rowl. Steell jun.		
18.6.1634	Robert Browne				Edward Greene		
10.4.1635	John Fawcus				Richard Bulman		
20.6.1634	John Pigdon				Thomas Colyer		
1.8.1632	Louvaine Rookeby				George Kirkeley		
1.8.1634	Robert Kell				Leonard Coulson		
3.10.1634	Thomas Grasshome				John Turpin		
1.9.1635	George Grasshome				John Turpin		
21.11.1634	Edward Durham				Michael Durham		
28.2.1634	Robert Collingwood				Michael Durham		
13.6.1633	John Allison				John Squire		
24.6.1633	Thomas Rowle				William Ogle		
4.9.1634	Thomas Wrangham				John Wrangham		
25.3.?	Leonard Chapling				John Wrangham		
24.3.1634	William Daglish				John Wrangham		
	John Bushbey				Christopher Cowen		

Date of indenture	Name of apprentice	Christian name of Father	Occupation of Father	Place of origin	Shipwright to whom apprenticed	Date of freedom	Price for freedom
9.6.1635	John Nicholson				Edmond Arrowsmith		
11.11.1635	Robert Steel				Thomas Steell		
10.11.1635	Rowland Selby				Leonard Coulson		
5.8.1633	Cuthbert Raine				John Carr		
30.4.1636	Michael Swann				Thomas Parker		
23.4.1636	Thomas Dining				William Ogle		
16.4.1636	Gilbert Steell				Rowland Steell		
12.5.1636	William Moody				William Steell		
1.2.1634	John Emmerson				Robert Gibson		
10.1.1635	Edward Rutter				Thomas Wilkinson		
20.6.1635	Henry Kellam	Mathew			George Jobling		
26.3.1635	Thomas Pringle				William Burrell		
9.8.1635	Thomas Prior				John Spurne		
9.12.1635	Anthony Bennett				Thomas Wade		
6.1.1634	George Hancock				Edward Greene		
21.9.1636	Henry Cooke				John Turpin		
28.12.1636	Robert Turner				George Turner		
2.2.1636	Robert Jobling				Ralph Jobling		
8.3.1636	John Watson				George Kirkeley		
3.2.1636	William Dods				Thomas Colyer		
10.5.1634	Thomas Swinburne				Roger Pearite		
9.8.1634	William Young				Edward Anderson		
27.6.1634	Ralph Boult				Edward Anderson		
23.12.1638	Edward Wilson				John Wrangham		
21.2.1636	Henry Watson				Robert Steell		
16.12.1635	William Forster				Rowland Seamer		
11.2.1636	John Armestrong				Thomas Wilkinson		
24.7.1635	James Watson				Edmond Arrowsmith		

Date of indenture	Name of apprentice	Christian name of Father	Occupation of Father	Place of origin	Shipwright to whom apprenticed	Date of freedom	Price for freedom
18.4.1638	Thomas Grame				William Burrell		
4.2.1637	John Cooke				George Turner		
18.4.1638	William Thompson				Edward Selby		
10.12.1631	Robert Cooke				Robert Cooke		
1.9.1635	Oswald Marshall				Thomas Steell		
31.12.1635	Anthony Bitleston	Thomas			Thomas Steell		
4.7.1637	Edward Forster	John			Thomas Steell		
31.5.1637	Thomas Robinson	Stephen			Robert Wilkinson		
20.6.1637	Robt Commyn	Anthony			Leonard Colson		
25.2.1636	Andrew Kirkley	Andrew			Robert Wailes		
30.5.1637	John Matland	John			William Steell		
2.2.1639	Mathew Tailer				John Harrison		
1.11.1638	Robert Fletcher				Thomas Ogle		
11.11.1637	George Steell				Christopher Knoks		
10.4.1639	Robt Chapman				Thomas Whaly		
5.7.1639	Roger Forster				Christopher Cowen		
29.6.1638	William Johnson				Peter Wilkinson		
11.11.1638	William Watt				Christopher Cowen		
11.7.1638	John Smith				George Cooke		
21.3.1639	Anthony Parkin				Richard Ewin		
2.2.1638	Edward Lorrane				Michael Durham		
24.11.1632	Robert Brantingham				John Colyer		
12.8.1633	George Begg				John Colyer		
1.5.1634	James Durham				John Colyer		
3.1.1636	Richard Turner				Thomas Colyer		
1.5.1638	George Greene				Edward Greene	1.12.1673	
1.5.1639	Robert Anderson				Jo. Wrangham		
2.2.1636	Mathew Tailor				John Harrison		

Date of indenture	Name of apprentice	Christian name of Father	Occupation of Father	Place of origin	Shipwright to whom apprenticed	Date of freedom	Price for freedom
8.6.1635	Lancelot Kitchen				Raiph Pattison		
24.6.1639	John Younge				Thomas Whaly		
21.5.1638	Tho. Robinson				Robert Wilkinson		
14.2.1637	Raiph Chambers				Robert Wilkinson		
1.9.1638	George Forster				Richard Bulman		
24.4.1638	John Armestrong				Thomas Wilkinson		
29.10.1639	John Young				William Burrell		
11.11.1639	Raiph Tailor				Christopher Newton		
18.9.1638	Francis Tideman				John Carr		
19.3.1639	Richard Thompson				George Cooke		
1.3.1639	Gilbert Hunter				George Turner	*	
3.8.1639	Math. Davison				John Frizell		
24.3.1639	Thomas Dixon				John Spurne		
24.1.1639	George Nicholson				Leonard Colson		
5.5.1640	John Stubs				Richard Midleton	*	
5.5.1640	Emanuell Kirkhouse				Roger Joblyn		
24.11.1640	Edmond Petite	John			John Ewin		
16.1.1641	Thomas Smith	Thomas			Edward Easterbie		
2.2.1639	John Wright	George			Edward Selby		
25.3.1641	Cuthbert Hartus	Wm			Christopher Bee	*	
8.4.1641	Jacob Stobbert	Cuthbert (decd)			John Poyde		
10.2.1640	John Earle	Thomas			George Kirkley		
20.3.1639	Thomas Barber	James			Edward Greene		
15.5.1641	John Snawball	John			Edward Greene		

* Indicates that the apprenticeship was not completed. The apprentice running away, or having his indentures formally cancelled. It would seem likely that this occurred in many instances but that the trouble to mark the register accordingly was not always taken.

Date of indenture	Name of apprentice	Christian name of Father	Occupation of Father	Place of origin	Shipwright to whom apprenticed	Date of freedom	Price for freedom
2.2.1640	Christopher Crosby	John			John Reay	*	
27.5.1641	George Huntley				John Carr		
27.5.1641	Gregorie Turner	Richard			John Carr		
9.4.1640	Henry Plumbton	Thomas			Thomas Wilkinson		
8.5.1641	Thomas Reay	John			Richard Midleton		
21.8.1641	Christopher Briggs				Wm Gamsbie		
23.6.1641	Robert Hudson	Thom.			Robert Brantingham		
1.[?] 1641	George Selby	Henry			Thomas Wrangham		
1.4.1641	Michaell Joplin	Michaell			George Joplin		
15.6.1641	Edm. Cooke		Yeoman		Robert Browne		
13.6.1641	Willm Coward	Martin			Robert Skeel		
3.6.1641	Raiph Tailor	Raiph			John Colyer		
5.10.1641	Charles Harle	Bartram			Edmond Arrowsmith		
11.11.1641	John Donkin	John			Roger Jobling		
9.11.1641	Robert Harrison	John			Rowland Steele jun.		
13.11.1641	William Shevill	George			Thomas Steele		
12.11.1641	Thomas Rutlish	Edward			George Kirkeley		
11.11.1641	George Tailor	Mathew			Edward Bullock		
10.4.1640	Robert Bowes	Robert			William Ogle		
20.6.1640	John Lowther	John			Robert Wilkinson		
24.6.1641	John Lumley	Arthur			Edw. Greene		
1.4.1641	John Watt	Patrick			Thomas Colyer		
8.11.1641	George Mark				Thomas Whaley		
20.10.1641	George Donnoldson	George			John Key		
9.11.1641	John Nicholson	Robert			Robert Wailes		
12.12.1641	Thomas Smith	Thomas			Robert Wailes		
11.11.1641	George Iley	William			Michael Durham	*	
28.12.1641	William Maddison	James			Thomas Steel		

Date of indenture	Name of apprentice	Christian name of Father	Occupation of Father	Place of origin	Shipwright to whom apprenticed	Date of freedom	Price for freedom
28.12.1641	Tho. Thompson	Henry			George Thompson		
12.1.1642	John Ogle	Marke			William Ogle		
26.6.1641	Thomas Heyns	John			Nicholas Atkinson		
5.2.1642	Thomas Dennis	Thomas			Henry Cooke		
21.2.1642	Henry Stintuer	Henry			Nicholas Atkinson		
9.4.1642	Geo. Cooke	Geo.			Peter Wilkinson		
19.2.1642	Roger Newton	John			Thomas Newton		
29.3.1642	Arthur Swann	Arthur			Michaell Durham		
27.3.1642	Andrew Bambrough	David			Robert Brantingham		
19.2.1642	James Reed	Tho.			Wm Steel		
10.2.1642	Cuthbert Burrell	Edward			Tho. Wrangham		
26.3.1642	Richard Atkinson	William			Geo. Dodgson		
20.12.1641	John Ramsey	Tho.			Leonard Colson		
3.5.1642	John Dobson	John			Richard Bulman		
27.5.1642	Michaell Armower	Tho.			Edward Selby		
2.6.1642	John Dixon	Alex.			Leonard Campling		
18.5.1642	William Douglas	William			William Burrell		
7.2.1642	Robert Briggs	John			Edward Easterby		
4.6.1642	Wm. Hutchinson	Willm			William Ogle		
24.6.1642	Raiph Dixon	Thomas			Christopher Bee		
20.8.1633	Richard Watson	Cuthbert			Raiph Pattison		
16.7.1642	John Spooner	Raiph			George West		
9.2.1643	Wm Crooke	John			Mathew Maddison		
24.6.1642	William Sidgwick	Tho.			Thomas Otway		
25.2.1643	Michael Thompson	Lawrance			John Reay	*	
18.6.1642	Cuthbert Newton	Tho.			Thomas Whaley		
1.5.1643	Martin Muscrop	Henry			Raiph Totherick		
2.2.1643	Raiph Turner	Richard			Thomas Rowls		

214

Date of indenture	Name of apprentice	Christian name of Father	Occupation of Father	Place of origin	Shipwright to whom apprenticed	Date of freedom	Price for freedom
1.8.1642	Robert Pearson	Wm			Geo. Cooke		
1.10.1644	Edmund Milburne	John			Robert Browne		
1.1.1644	Robt Bowdon	Oswold			John Wrangham		
22.5.1643	Tho. Adamson	Tho.			Leonard Colson		
11.11.1644	John Pigdon	John			Tho. Colyer		
26.12.1644	Luke Hutton	George			Tho. Colyer		
26.12.1644	Geo. Ogle	Tho.			Tho. Ogle		
1.1.1645	Geo. Morton	John			John Key		
11.11.1641	Wm Liddell	James			Edmond Arrowsmith	*	
8.2.1645	John Otterington				Thomas Wrangham		
18.2.1645	Raiph Parkins	Tho.			Tho. Wilkinson		
1.3.1645	John Smith	Tho.			Wm Lawson		
17.3.1645	John Precious	George			John Nicholson		
25.4.1645	John Farbrick	John			Tho. Steel		
1.4.1645	Wm Lawson	Andrew			Rich. Bulman		
9.4.1645	David Skeel	Rich.			Robt Skeel		
15.5.1645	Robt Jackson	John			Cuthbert Backworth		
26.5.1645	John Wilkinson				Philip Wilkinson	*	
11.11.1639	John Sparrow				James Colyer		
1.8.1645	Raiph Kellett				William Ogle		
27.9.1645	Rowland Newton	Christopher			Christopher Newton		
4.1.1645	James Butler	John			Geo. Turner		
7.10.1645	Henry Earle	Thomas			Willm Rasbrough		
11.11.1645	Cuthbert Hunter	John			Tho. Wilkinson		
22.9.1645	Robt Pearson				John Ewins		
16.5.1643	Mathew Reed				Cuthbert Raine		
11.11.1645	James Swinbourne				John Poyd		
1.9.1645	Geo. Watt	Patrick			Robert Skeel		

215

Date of indenture	Name of apprentice	Christian name of Father	Occupation of Father	Place of origin	Shipwright to whom apprenticed	Date of freedom	Price for freedom
1.1.1646	William Potts	Tho.			Tho. Cooke		
27.12.1645	Cuthbert Woodman	Anthony			Tho. Wilkinson		
27.2.1646	Tho. Richardson	Anthony			Robt Davison		
8.2.1646	Anthony Bourdas				Rowland Steel		
16.2.1646	Barthram Nicholson	Mathew			Leo. Colson		
2.3.1646	Tho. Erratt				Henry Cooke jun.		
2.2.1646	Richard Wallas				Roger Lumley		
1.5.1646	John Smith				William Burrell		
20.4.1646	Ambrose Preston				Geo. Kirkley		
23.5.1646	John Kelett				Robt Brantingham		
25.3.1646	Roger Kirtlin				Cuthbert Raine		
29.9.1646	Thomas Forster	Wm			Edward Selby	27.12.1674	£2 2 4
26.11.1646	Henry Hedley	Thomas			Peter Wilkinson		
17.10.1646	Geo. Brough	Tho.			William Rosbrough		
1.6.1646	Tho. Jackson	John			Henry Cooke		
11.11.1646	Willm Gibson	Roland			Edward Wilson		
2.9.1646	Nicholas Ridley	Willm			Cuthbert Backworth		
29.9.1646	Robert Wilkinson	John			Michael Durham		
1.3.1647	Tho. Watt	Patrick			John Key		
3.2.1647	William Frame	Roger			Michael Durham		
16.3.1646	Wm Trewhit				John Wrangham		
11.11.1646	Richard Wilson	Willm			John Wrangham		
25.3.1647	Francis Greene	Willm			Edward Greene		
10.2.1647	Wm Chester	Christopher			Hen. Cooke		
1.5.1647	Jeremie Woodhouse				Leonard Camplin		
3.7.1647	Roger Murton				Thomas Otway		
26.7.1647	Francis Fetherstonhaugh				John Key		
16.5.1642	Charles Greene				John Carr		

216

Date of indenture	Name of apprentice	Christian name of Father	Occupation of Father	Place of origin	Shipwright to whom apprenticed	Date of freedom	Price for freedom
3.8.1647	Andrew Longstaffe	John			Wm Forster		
3.11.1647	Tho. Robinson	John			John Watson		
25.12.1647	Robert Scott	Mathew			Willm Lawson		
5.2.1648	John Tailor	Oswold			Mathew Tailor		
29.1.1648	Thos. Harrison	Patrick			Tho. Atkinson		
30.3.1648	Edward Dixon	Thomas			Nichol. Atkinson		
25.5.1648	Wm Pallacer	John			Edward Greene		
2.2.1649	Gamaliel Wood	Joseph			George Greene		
5.3.1647	Francis Rogers	Nicholas	Gent	Durham	George Greene		
24.1.1649	John Watson	Wm	Yeoman	Anick [Alnwick]	Peter Wilkinson		
16.1.1649	Antho. Nicholson	Richard (decd)			Tho. Wrangham		
22.2.1649	Richard Smith				Michaell Durham		
25.5.1648	Wm Pallaser	Tho.	Baker & Beire brewer	Newcastle			
28.4.1649	Edward Shaftoe	Tho.			Edward Greene		
11.5.1649	John Bowman	Leon.			John Spurne		
1.5.1649	Ralph Wilson	Wm			John Trewhitt		
16.5.1649	Robert Wood	Symond			Tho. Wrangham		
16.5.1649	Micha. Falcon	Henry			Tho. Ogle		
5.7.1648	Tho. Wallis	Geo.			Tho. Colyer		
8.9.1649	Cuthbert Ogle	Mark			Leon. Colson		
19.10.1649	Tho. Emmerson	Robt			Robt Wailes	†	
25.2.1650	Nicho. Dent	Christo.			Geo. Kirkley		
2.7.1649	John Cooke	John		Bridlington	Henry Cooke jun.		
1.4.1650	John Shaftoe	Henry			Micha. Durham		

† Indicates that the entry is marked to the effect that the apprentice died before completing his indentures.

217

Date of indenture	Name of apprentice	Christian name of Father	Occupation of Father	Place of origin	Shipwright to whom apprenticed	Date of freedom	Price for freedom
24.5.1650	Antho. Hall	Nicho.			Leo. Colson		
5.5.1650	Tho. Wilkinson	Willm			Tho. Atkinson		
3.6.1650	John Nicholson	Mathew			Geo. Nicholson		
11.6.1650	Robert Watson	Tho.			George Kirkley		
27.4.1650	Samuel Newton	Henry			Christopher Bee		
1.1.1649	Geo. Selby	John			Tho. Pattison		
1.8.1650	George Wetherhead	James			Robert Turner		
11.11.1650	Antho. Parrat				Roger Harbottle		
14.10.1650	John Harle				Charles Harle		
23.1.1651	Peter Forster	Robert			John Wrangham		
2.4.1651	William Day	Bartram			Roger Hudson		
1.4.1651	Robert Harrigate	James			John Young		
1.5.1651	Tho. Bell	John			James Durham		
4.3.1651	John Milbourne	William			John Nicholson		
24.5.1651	Raiph Dick	John			Nicho. Atkinson		
23.6.1651	Robt Gallowley	Nicholas			Rowland Steel		
2.7.1651	Raiph Anderson	Raiph			John Poid		
26.2.1652	Edward Earl	Thomas			George Cooke		
17.7.1651	Thomas Comin	Christo.			Roger Forster		
1.6.1651	Leonard Middleton	Richard			Henry Cooke		
18.8.1651	Willm Browne	Robert			John Snawball		
4.9.1651	Robt Mitford	Gawine			Robert Brantingham		
30.5.1651	Raiph Pickering	Walter			John Spurne		
11.11.1651	John Lockey	Bartram			Henry Cooke sen.		
20.11.1651	William Wilkinson	Willm			Richard Turner		
8.12.1651	Henry Juman	Tobias			Roger Hudson		
29.12.1651	Raiph Thew	Wm			Mathew Tailor		
2.2.1652	Wm Chapman	Wm			Wm Rosebrough	*	

Date of indenture	Name of apprentice	Christian name of Father	Occupation of Father	Place of origin	Shipwright to whom apprenticed	Date of freedom	Price for freedom
2.2.1652	Charles Harvie	Charles			Tho. Colyer		
9.2.1652	Antho. Kirkley	George			John Watson		
1.8.1651	Antho. Nicholson	John			Cuthbert Raine		
1.1.1652	Mathew Hutchinson	John			Cuthbert Raine		
26.12.1651	Robt Ogle	Robt			Willm Harrison		
8.3.1652	John Yallowley	Robt			James Durham		
18.3.1652	Wm Cowle	Wm			Tho. Wrangham		
14.2.1652	Raiph Coward	Geo.			Tho. Pattison		
2.3.1652	John Crawforth	Hen.			John Reay		
2.3.1652	John Alanson	Robt			Cuthbert Backworth	*	
16.3.1652	Nicho. Hopper				Cuthbert Backworth		
10.3.1652	Cuthbert Bone				Robt Skeell		
2.2.1652	John Chambers				Edward Greene		
1.4.1652	Raiph Thompson				Tho. Colyer		
1.4.1652	John Little				Thomas Atkinson		
4.10.1651	Wm Wallis				John Ewin		
8.5.1652	Henry Lawson	Hector			John Reay		
1.5.1652	Thomas Watson	Tho.			John Watson		
3.5.1652	Thomas Fenwick	Michael			Robert Davison		
7.6.1652	Raiph Emmerson	George			John Snawball		
31.1.1652	Robert Quarier	Mathew			Roger Forster		
24.6.1652	Antho. Lawson	Alex.			Roger Jobling	27.12.1692	£2 7 7
28.9.1652	George Hall	Andrew			Robert Wales		
25.3.1652	Lancelot Ogle	Mark			George Nicholson		
9.6.1652	John Young	George			John Young		
16.3.1653	Cuthbert Smith	Cuthbert			Tho. Wilkinson		
30.9.1652	Cuthbert Wiley	Antho.			Edward Selby		
11.11.1652	Henry Forster	Tho.			William Thompson	*	

Date of indenture	Name of apprentice	Occupation of Father	Christian name of Father	Place of origin	Shipwright to whom apprenticed	Date of freedom	Price for freedom
21.12.1652	John Turner		David		John Nicholson		
4.2.1653	Willm Wilkinson		John		James Durham		
19.3.1653	John Wilkinson		John		Leonard Colson		
11.11.1652	Willm Ramsey				Willm Rosbrough		
22.6.1653	Edward Dod		John		Edward Wilson		
1.11.1653	Roger Lomley		George		Roger Lomley		
1.10.1653	Thomas Courtis		Thomas		George Turner		
19.10.1653	Willm Brayson		Willm		Roger Forster		
24.12.1653	Robert Turner				Willm Thompson		
29.9.1653	Martin Earle				Wm Rosebrough		
24.1.1654	Michaell Auckland				Arthur Swann		
16.2.1652	Cuthbert Smith				Thom. Wilkinson		
12.2.1653	George Wilkinson				Thom. Wilkinson		
6.8.1653	John Johnson				Thom. Wilkinson		
9.3.1654	Luke Moffet		John		Michael Durham		
28.4.1654	Ralph Elsdon		John		Rowland Steele	27.12.1673	£2 5 5
9.6.1654	John Walker		Alex.		Rowland Steele		
30.5.1654	Tho. Bowden		Robert		Edward Greene		
7.6.1652	Robert French		Tho.		Robert Brantingham		
20.5.1654	Cuthbert Thew		Ralph		John Trewhitt		
21.6.1654	John Fish		Cuthbert		Willm Potts		
18.8.1654	Willm Bootiman		Willm		Christo. Bee		
28.9.1654	George Nixon		John		Nicho. Atkinson		
14.8.1654	Ralph Fetherstonhaugh		Geo.		John Reay	*	
24.8.1654	Tho. Jackson		Jervis		Henry Cooke		
	John Lee		Geo.		Cuthbert Backworth		
24.11.1654	Henry Dunn		Tho.		George Turner		
26.12.1654	James Burne		Tho.		John Pigdon		

Date of indenture	Name of apprentice	Christian name of Father	Occupation of Father	Place of origin	Shipwright to whom apprenticed	Date of freedom	Price for freedom
11.11.1654	John Reed	Percival			John Wright	*	
29.12.1654	John Chaitor	Cuthbert			Thomas Thompson	†	
8.1.1655	George Smith	James			Geo. Durham		
27.12.1654	Willm Woodman	Antho.			Cuthbert Woodman		
19.2.1655	John Richardley	George			Edward Milbourne	27.12.1678	
3.2.1655	Philip Story	Ambrose			Edward Greene		
2.2.1655	George Williamson	John			George Tailor		
16.4.1655	Anthony Wilkinson	John			John Wilkinson		
2.2.1655	Theophilus Smith	William			Robert Davison	†	
[?].2.1655	Thomas Reed	Tho.			Willm Forster		
27.3.1655	John Chirniside	Richard			William Watt		
1.3.1655	Robert Nicholson	Mathew			Barthram Nicholson		
1.5.1655	Henry Allison	Mathew			John Watson		
1.5.1655	Peter Cuthbert	Robert			George Greene		
1.5.1655	Gawine Cole	Alexander			Robert Anderson		
19.4.1655	George Waugh	John			George Dodshon		
1.5.1655	Jeremiah Fenic	Anthoney			Cuthbert Hunter	†	
12.5.1655	John Saburne	Richard			Henry Cooke sen.		
1.6.1655	George Browne	Robert			Heugh Colyer		
10.5.1655	Robert Scott	Richard			Ambrose Preston		
6.5.1652	John Davison	Gawine			Roger Harbottle		
11.11.1654	Geo. Selbie	Willm			John Ewin		
31.5.1655	George Wallis	Geo.			Ralph Parkin		
4.6.1655	Ralph Robson	James			George Cooke		
[?].5.1655	John Cuthbert	Ralph			George Mourton		
23.6.1655	Tho. Newland	Peter			Edward Lorraine		
28.6.1655	John Bradey	Christo.			Robert Wales		
21.6.1655	Wm Bell	Wm			Mathew Tailor		

Date of indenture	Name of apprentice	Christian name of Father	Occupation of Father	Place of origin	Shipwright to whom apprenticed	Date of freedom	Price for freedom
12.7.1655	Barnard Cuthbert	Robert			John Snawball		
25.8.1655	Gilbert Stanley	Henry			Edward Selby	27.12.1676	£2 9 2
18.6.1655	John Easterby	Richard			John Trewhitt		
26.6.1655	John Knaggs	Alexander			Thomas Blunt		
1.10.1655	John Thompson	Ralph			Willm Thompson		
5.10.1655	Henry Robinson	Henry			Willm Harrison		
10.11.1655	Richard Thew	John			George Tailor		
18.10.1655	John Wilson	John			George Nicholson		
14.11.1655	Patrick Dixon	Ralph			Robert Bowdon	*	
1.10.1655	Roger Richardson	Thomas			Laurence Rooksby	†	
1.8.1655	William Walker	Robert			Willm Burrell		
1.11.1655	John Hooper	Robert			Francis Rogers		
1.1.1656	John Gray	Thomas			Robert Davison	*	
1.11.1655	Willm Alwin	Edward			John Reay		
18.1.1656	Robert Simpson	John			Tho. Wrangham		
5.1.1656	Claudius Reay	Claudius			John Smith		
2.2.1656	William Smith	Tho.			Francis Rogers		
11.2.1656	Mathew Wake	Richard			William Rosebrough		
24.2.1656	John Moore	Willm			Michaell Durham		
29.1.1656	John Wilkinson	William			Thomas Atkinson		
14.1.1656	Francis Hipson	Tho.			John Nicholson		
3.2.1656	William Chaitor	Robert			Andrew Forster		
28.2.1656	Michaell Ward	Cuthbert			Geo. Durham	*	
13.3.1656	Robert Johnson	John			Jacob Stobbert		
8.2.1656	Willm Killingworth	Lancelot			William Shevill		
13.2.1656	Robert Hall	John			William Harrison		
26.2.1656	Lionell Mures	Michaell			Robert Collingwood	25.7.1689	
1.1.1656	Thomas Manuell	Edward			John Pigdon	†	

222

Date of indenture	Name of apprentice	Christian name of Father	Occupation of Father	Place of origin	Shipwright to whom apprenticed	Date of freedom	Price for freedom
25.3.1656	Willm Simpson	Thomas			Mathew Tailor		
12.3.1656	Tho. Swalwell	John			Cuthbert Hunter	*	
3.4.1656	William Cartington	Gawine			Tho. Steele		
25.3.1656	George Snawball	Tho.			Tho. Steele		
4.4.1656	Edward Slaitor	Richard			Ambrose Preston		
2.2.1656	Edward Wolfe	Richard			John Wilkinson		
2.1.1656	William Earle	George			Tho. Parkinson		
20.4.1656	Luke Cooke	Richard			John Wright		
28.4.1656	George Hutchinson	John			Robert Turner		
1.5.1656	Nicholas Kell	Edward			Thomas Spourne		
1.5.1656	Wm Young	Stephen			Rowland Kirkley		
24.4.1656	Edward Milbourne	Edward			Edward Lorraine	*	
17.5.1656	Robt Hopper	John			Edward Greene		
24.5.1656	Robt Fleck	George			Francis Greene	27.12.1676	£2 6 6
1.5.1656	George Thompson	Tho.			John Smith		
1.5.1656	Tho. Lyddell	George			Henry Hedley		
1.5.1656	Richard Nicholson	John			Mathew Reed		
26.5.1656	George Wills	John			George Mourton		
23.4.1656	John Young	Geo.			John Lowther		
31.5.1656	George Whitfeild	Robert			Edward Greene jun.		
4.6.1656	Thomas Atkinson	Nicholas			Cuthbert Woodman	25.7.1689	
4.6.1656	Robert Todd	John			Bartram Nicholson		
9.6.1656	Ralph Robson	James			Robert Turner	*	
17.6.1656	Robert Thompson	Arthur			Thomas Robinson		
18.6.1656	Stephen Brewhouse	John			Robert Bowdon		
18.9.1656	John Archbould	Wm			John Young	*	
17.9.1656	Wm Selby	John			John Ewins	*	
13.9.1656	Willm Johnson	Robt			Thomas Wrangham	*	

223

Date of indenture	Name of apprentice	Christian name of Father	Occupation of Father	Place of origin	Shipwright to whom apprenticed	Date of freedom	Price for freedom
9.8.1656	John Neesebet	Philip			Charles Harle	*	
3.11.1656	Thomas Walker	Alexander			Thomas Steele	29.12.1690	
5.7.1656	George Kell	Edward			Peter Turner	†	
24.12.1656	Andrew Spoore	Andrew			Tho. Wallis	†	
30.6.1656	Willm Gibson	Thomas			John Earle	†	
4.12.1656	John Thompson	Ralph			Ralph Parkin		
30.1.1657	Lancelot Swanston	Richard			Averey Wrangham	†	
28.1.1657	Tho. Peacock	Tho.			Richard Wallis		
1.10.1656	John Hunter	Thomas			Thomas Forster	*	
23.2.1657	Ralph James	John			Mathew Reede	†	
5.2.1657	John Wilkinson	John			Robert Wilkinson		
14.2.1657	Robert Jobson	Robert			Arthur Swan	free n.d.	
17.3.1657	John Letteney	John			Francis Greene		
31.3.1657	Oswold Young	John			John Tailor	*	
1.5.1656	Christopher Middleton	Tho.			Thomas Ogle		
20.4.1656	Thomas Gibson	Thomas			Wm Potts		
5.8.1657	James Moffet	John			George Durham	†	
23.11.1657	Leonard Gill	James			John Young		
3.10.1657	James Nicholson	John			His father	†	
29.3.1658	Thomas Peirson	William			Robert Peirson		
1.5.1658	Ralph Gibson	George			Thomas Wrangham		
6.5.1658	Richard Richardson	Henry			Michaell Durham		
23.10.1658	Wm Cooke				George Cooke sen.		
1.2.1659	John Walker				John Pigdon	*	
28.12.1658	Anthony Hall				Anthony Hall		
11.11.1658	Henry Richardson				Edward Selby	†	
7.3.1659	Wm Cutter	John			John Nicholson		
5.3.1659	John Smith	John			Anthony Hall		

Date of indenture	Name of apprentice	Christian name of Father	Occupation of Father	Place of origin	Shipwright to whom apprenticed	Date of freedom	Price for freedom
2.5.1659	John Parkin	Tho.			Tho. Atkinson		
24.5.1659	John Holme	Henry			Cuthbert Hunter	†	
1.7.1659	William Johnson	William			John Watson		
8.7.1659	Stephen Johnson	Robt			Avara Wrangham		
5.9.1659	Thomas Foxton	Wm			Edward Greene	*	
2.6.1660	Henry Best	Tho.			Tho. Wrangham		
3.2.1660	Michael Atkinson	Tho.			Edward Greene		
25.4.1660	Tho. Shaw	Willm			Henry Cooke		
16.11.1659	Francis Watson	Nicho.			Henry Cooke		
1.3.1660	John Dent	Christo.			Nicholas Dent		
16.10.1660	Tho. Wilson	John			John Ewins		
1.3.1661	John Wallis	John			George Nicholson		
27.3.1661	John Haton	Tho.			Robert Brantingham	†	
29.9.1661	Ralph Haggerston	Geo.			Ralph Anderson		
10.10.1661	Tho. Story	Tho.			Wm Coward	28.3.1676	£2 6 6
5.7.1661	Richard Wilkinson	Alex.			Michaell Durham	†	
14.4.1662	George Wetherburn	John			Thomas Wrangham	*	
2.2.1663	George Nicholson	John			Thomas Wrangham	27.12.1676	£2 3 3
10.3.1663	George Browne	William			Avery Wrangham		
1.1.1663	William Eggleston	John			John Watson		
26.3.1663	John Husband	John			Edward Green	26.4.1698	£2 2 2
21.3.1662	Tho. Thackway	Willm			Cuthbert Bone	27.12.1673	£2 7 0
1.7.1663	Marke Greene	Mark			John Wright	†	
5.8.1661	Christo. Richardson				John Tailor		
21.5.1663	Gilbert Sanderson	Archbald			Willm Thompson		
29.9.1663	Willm Claton	John			Roland Kirkley	†	
8.10.1663	Willm Archbold	Geo.			Charles Harle		
26.10.1663	Tho. Clough	Thomas			Thomas Steel	27.12.1673	£2 2 2

Date of indenture	Name of apprentice	Christian name of Father	Occupation of Father	Place of origin	Shipwright to whom apprenticed	Date of freedom	Price for freedom
1.8.1663	Robert Dunn	Thomas (decd)			Peter Greene		
13.1.1663	Tho. Lyddell	Thomas			Willm Potts		
8.2.1658	George Stoddart	Wm			Tho. Pattison		
15.9.1663	Tho. Downaby	Edward			Michael Auckland	†	
8.12.1663	Abra. Eden	Robt			Francis Greene		
11.2.1662	Robt Cuthbert	Wm			Francis Greene		
1.2.1664	George Jackson	Charles			Henry Cooke		
25.7.[?]	George Redshaw	George			Cuthbert Woodman		
29.12.1663	Robt Acklam	Robt			Edward Greene		
18.1.1664	Edward Fall	Robt			Ralph Parkin		
22.4.1663	Wm Lawson	Tho.			George Nicholson	*	
18.3.1664	Geo. Tailor	Tho.			Francis Greene	*	
16.1.1662	Philip Wilkinson	John			John Wilkinson jun.		
19.5.1662	Michael Wilkinson	John			Cuthbert Smyth		
26.3.1664	Wm Tailor	Willm			Cuthbert Smyth		
3.2.1662	John Backworth	John			Cuthbert Backworth	27.12.1679	£2 8 9
14.12.1663	James Atkinson	Tho.			Cuthbert Backworth		
24.4.1664	Robert Johnson	Robert			Cuthbert Backworth		
20.5.1664	Malachie Otley	Michael			Peter Greene	28.12.1674	£2 7 7
23.6.1664	Lancelot Buston	Willm			Roland Kirkley	†	
23.1.1664	Thomas Fletcher	Nicholas			Cuthbert Hunter	27.12.1686	£2 2 10
21.5.1662	Roger Fawcus	Lancelot			Cuthbert Hunter		
10.3.1663	Robert Ward	Francis			Thomas Poyd		
1.6.1664	Ralph Coutsie	Wm			Robert Bowdon		
2.2.1663	James Mosman	John			Willm Rosbrough		
1.8.1664	John Hopper	Cuthbert			Andrew Forster	†	
9.4.1664	John Moore	Thomas			Roger Forster	†	

Date of indenture	Name of apprentice	Christian name of Father	Occupation of Father	Place of origin	Shipwright to whom apprenticed	Date of freedom	Price for freedom
9.12.1664	Ralph Merriman	Tho.			John Snawball	29.9.1674	£2 8 8
9.2.1665	Ralph Spoore	Ralph			Michael Durham	27.12.1677	£2 2 2
1.1.1665	Cuthbert Greene	Willm			John Lockey	2.2.1674	£2 6 6
25.4.1665	Martin Chaitor	Cuthbert			Thomas Thompson	2.2.1673	£5 4 6
16.5.1665	Robert Smyth	John			William Rosbrough		
29.6.1665	John Morton	John			John Snawball	29.9.1694	£2 18 8
1.2.1666	Tho. Dixon	Willm			John Watson		
1.1.1667	Richard Milner				Francis Greene	†	
26.3.1666	John Kipling	Richard			John Harrison	29.1.1690	£2 16 0
1.5.1666	Henry Wrangham	Willm			Thomas Wrangham	22.4.1679	£2 10 3
9.4.1666	Edward Downaby	Edward			Wm Lawson	†	
12.4.1666	Willm Duck	Willm			Wm Lawson	*	
8.3.1666	John Turner	George			George Nicholson		
1.3.1666	Thomas Rogerson	Willm			Avara Wrangham	*	
16.6.1666	Robt Sadler	Cuthbert			Charles Harle		
2.2.1666	James Betson	John			Cuthbert Bone		
5.9.1666	Thomas Brewhouse	Thomas			Avera Wrangham	†	
1.1.1667	Andrew Trumble	Robert			Henry Cooke	*	
1.12.1666	Joseph Letany	John			John Letany	*	
3.5.1667	George Rownethwait	Willm		Sunderland	Thomas Steele	†	
22.5.1667	Wm Wilkinson	Richard			Edward Greene		
1.5.1667	Thomas Bailey	Thomas			John Watson		
1.6.1667	Thomas Salkeld	William			Mathew Hutchinson	6.4.1675	£2 2 2
17.10.1667	Thomas Hutson	Richard			Willm Rosbrough	29.9.1677	£2 2 2
21.1.1668	John Milbourne	John			John Milbourne	27.12.1676	£2 3 9
2.2.1668	Willm Emmott	George			John Colyer		
5.2.1668	Thomas Stainsby	John			Mathew Reed		
20.2.1668	Willm Fishirk	Willm			Thomas Peacock	†	

227

Date of indenture	Name of apprentice	Christian name of Father	Occupation of Father	Place of origin	Shipwright to whom apprenticed	Date of freedom	Price for freedom
24.2.1668	Robert Jopling	Willm			Robert Jopling	29.9.1677	£2 2 2
2.3.1668	Nicholas Browne	Nicholas			Mathew Reed	27.12.1681	£2 10 10
11.5.1668	John Robson	Hector			John Chambers		
13.5.1668	Tho. Pigg	John			Ambrose Preston		
15.6.1668	Willm Charlton	Cuthbert			Thomas Ogle		
6.7.1668	Robt Watson	Oswold			Willm Shevill		
22.9.1668	Thomas Hodshon	John			John Letaney	†	
1.7.1668	John Rownethwait	William			Henry Cooke	†	
7.9.1668	John Rookeby	Ralph			Lawrance Rookeby	27.12.1676	£2 4 10
10.8.1668	Henry Watson	John			Rowland Kirkley		
13.10.1668	Clement Burton	Thomas			George Nicholson		
15.6.1663	John Reed	Raiph			Willm Forster	free n.d.	
20.1.1669	Thomas Eagleston	John			Nicholas Dent	*	
2.2.1669	Nicho. Smith				Thomas Peacock	†	
12.2.1669	Ralph Small				Thomas Atkinson jun.	22.4.1679	£2 6 6
22.2.1669	Jonathan Thew				Robt Davison		
23.2.1669	John Arkelah				Tho. Spurne	27.12.1684	
25.3.1669	Thomas Welford				Peter Greene		
6.3.1669	Willm Jackson				Mathew Hutchinson		
19.3.1669	Walter Elliott				Willm Lawson	†	
15.7.1668	James Tweddell				Anthoney Wilkinson		
16.4.1669	Ralph Gourely	Wm			John Cooke	*	
12.5.1669	Charles Garrett	Thomas			Roland Kirkley		
20.4.1669	John Unthank	Ralph			Tho. Fenwick	27.12.1676	£2 4 4
3.5.1669	John Wallas	George			Tho. Fenwick	*	£2 4 4
1.5.1669	Ralph Greene	Willm			John Lockey	27.12.1678	
1.5.1669	John Greeneley	John			Henry Hedley		

Date of indenture	Name of apprentice	Christian name of Father	Occupation of Father	Place of origin	Shipwright to whom apprenticed	Date of freedom	Price for freedom
3.5.1669	Robert Smallpage	Robt			Tho. Wrangham jun.		
13.7.1669	Charles Wailes	Robert			His father		
30.6.1669	Robert Silvertopp	Oswould			Richard Thew	27.12.1681	£2 10 10
20.9.1669	James Langland	Thomas			Thomas Wrangham jun.	5.6.1677	£2 4 4
2.6.1669	George Robson	Simond			Cuth. Bone	22.4.1679	£2 9 0
13.7.1669	Henry Brantingham	Nathaniel			Wm Watt		
11.6.1669	John Clugh	Martin			Robert Simson	27.4.1677	£2 3 4
10.9.1669	Wm Morley	George			John Cook		
1.6.1669	Henry Rennoldson	Stephen			Robert Hopper	27.12.1676	£2 4 4
21.9.1669	John Poyd	Alexander			Thomas Forster	21.12.1691	£2 13 0
9.7.1669	Robert Murton	Henry		Blaydon	Raiph Thew		
11.5.1668	John Robson	Hector	Yeoman	Tinemouth	John Chambers		
30.6.1669	George Bowe	John	Shipwright	Sunderland	Tho. Steele	†	
5.10.1669	Tho. Lattany	Tho.			John Lattany	2.4.1678	
14.1.1670	William Browne	John			John Watson	22.4.1679	£2 3 9
4.2.1670	John Goodson	Richard			Michael Durham	27.12.1678	£2 5 5
28.12.1669	James Glenn	James			Wm Brason	25.7.1689	£2 5 5
22.1.1670	Gawine Robinson	Michael		Ongham	Wm Coward		
1.2.1670	Math. Newton	John			Wm Gibson		
24.1.1670	Anthony Chambers	Raiph			His father		
16.8.1669	Roger Grey	Andrew			Rich. Wallas		
1.5.1663	Richard Clark	Rich.			Rich. Wallas		
13.5.1668	John Wallas	Rich.		Cockfeild	His father	29.9.1693	£2 2 2
15.2.1670	William Park	William			Tho. Wrangham	27.12.1677	£2 2 2
11.11.1663	George Darnton	George			Francis Rogers	†	
3.3.1670	Fran. Hawman	Andrew			Francis Rogers	*	
30.3.1670	John Cafferton	John			Tho. Wilson		

229

Date of indenture	Name of apprentice	Christian name of Father	Occupation of Father	Place of origin	Shipwright to whom apprenticed	Date of freedom	Price for freedom
14.2.1670	Stephen Hopper	Stephen			Roger Forster	*	
29.3.1670	Robert Waugh	Bartho.			Roger Forster		
2.4.1670	Edward Lawson	Robert			Robert Lawson		
30.4.1670	Lancelot Humble	John			Wm Gibson		
7.5.1670	Rich. Peirson	Tho.		Northumberland	Avara Wrangham		
6.4.1670	Robert Fenwick	Roger			Robert Hopper		
13.4.1670	Jeremiah Gillery	Tho.			John Harrison		
22.11.1669	Thomas Potts	Clement			William Bootiman		
6.1.1669	John Spoore	John			George Tailor	27.12.1676	£2 4 4
30.5.1668	Nicholas Raine	John			George Tailor	29.9.1676	£2 3 3
2.5.1670	Geo. Chaitor	Cuthbert			Tho. Thompson	27.12.1677	£2 3 4
14.4.1670	Henry Browne	George			Nicholas Kell	28.2.1685	£2 2 2
1.7.1669	Francis Burdon	Mathew			Cuthbert Hunter	4.10.1686	£2 12 2
21.5.1670	Robert Lowes	Lancelot			Ralph Wilson	*	
13.2.1669	John Hodshon	John			Francis Greene	*	
26.2.1669	John Storey	John			Tho. Atkinson		
26.2.1669	Thomas Leyburne	Wm			Tho. Atkinson	*	
1.5.1668	John Trewhitt	John			Tho. Atkinson		
24.5.1670	Luke Storey	Rich.			Henry Earle		
30.9.1669	Raiph Reed	Thomas			Thomas Reed	†	
5.10.1669	Elias Robson	Elias	Gent	Clifton nr. York	Tho. Reed		
30.4.1670	William Potter	James			George Nicholson	27.12.1678	£2 5 5
25.5.1670	Thomas Johnson	John			Edward Greene	27.12.1683	
23.5.1670	William Wenington	James			George Wilkinson		
30.5.1670	Thomas Dunlap	Alex.			George Wilkinson		
9.9.1668	John Tailor	John			Wm Potts	*	
27.4.1669	Thomas Forster	Thomas			Wm Potts	*	
17.4.1669	Thomas Lyddell	John			Wm Potts	*	

Date of indenture	Name of apprentice	Christian name of Father	Occupation of Father	Place of origin	Shipwright to whom apprenticed	Date of freedom	Price for freedom
25.6.1670	Tho. Welford	Tho.			Wm Hunter	29.9.1692	£2 14 1
10.2.1670	John Hall	John			Cuthbert Beckworth		
25.7.1670	Geo. Wright	Mathew			Robert Davison jun.		
2.8.1670	William Thomson	Raiph			John Milbourne		
1.10.1668	Tho. Ramsey	Cuthbert			Thomas Poyd		
4.6.1669	Stephen Fowler	Mich.			Thomas Poyd		
7.6.1670	William Tinkler	Michael			John Lumley		
25.3.1670	James Gillery	Richard			Gamaliel Wood		
3.8.1670	John Bee	William			Robert Lawson		
24.6.1670	Henry Strother	Henry			Cuthbert Bone		
21.9.1670	Geo. Forster	Thomas			Andrew Forster	27.12.1688	
2.11.1670	Tho. Barber	Tho.			John Collyer	24.6.1679	£2 6 6
28.12.1666	Tho. Stobbart	Tho.			John Beckworth		
3.5.1668	Christopher Gillery	Richard			John Beckworth	18.4.1682	£2 7 7
11.11.1670	Tho. Hall	Andrew			Raiph Featherston		
26.12.1670	Nicholas Rutter	John			Wm Chaitor	*	
30.9.1670	William Bullock	Tristram			Tho. Ogle		
1.5.1669	William Pattison	John			The Company of Shipwrights		
19.1.1671	Geo. Nicholson	Wm			Mathew Reed		
9.3.1666	Robert Stainsby	John			Wm Wilkinson	†	
1.4.1668	Tho. Bolron	John			Wm Wilkinson	*	
28.6.1670	Richard Dawson	Robert			William Bootyman	27.12.1677	£2 2 2
23.3.1671	Charles Simpson	Charles			Ralph Parkin		
24.2.1671	Tho. Campling				Thomas Gibson	22.4.1679	£2 4 4
14.2.1671	Andrew Dawson	Thomas			John Collyer	24.6.1678	£2 2 0
20.2.1671	Edward Lumsdell	Ralph			William Brason		
2.2.1671	Richard Cotes	William			Roger Durham	29.9.1680	£2 2 2

231

Date of indenture	Name of apprentice	Christian name of Father	Occupation of Father	Place of origin	Shipwright to whom apprenticed	Date of freedom	Price for freedom
6.2.1671	George Carr	William			Thomas Wailes	27.12.1689	£2 3 3
1.3.1671	Richard Richardson	Geo.			William Rosbrough	21.6.1680	£2 5 5
20.4.1671	William Boyes	Bulmer			Henry Cooke	*	
1.5.1671	Lancelott Newton	John			Thomas Spurne		
1.4.1671	Thomas Mawr	Thomas			John Wilkinson		
31.12.1670	Christopher Blackbeard	Christopher			Cuthbert Beckwith		
24.6.1671	Marmaduke Smithson	John			Raiph Gibson	28.12.1685	£2 2 2
14.6.1671	Michaell Johnson	Lancelot			Martin Earle	27.12.1678	£2 4 4
26.4.1671	John Wilkinson	John			Peter Greene		
12.6.1671	John Swallwell	George			Peter Greene	29.9.1677	£2 2 2
6.5.1671	John Wright	William			John Wright		
25.1.1671	George Haslipp	Robert			Cuthbert Hunter	†	
20.6.1671	William Strother	Cuthbert			Henry Cooke		
7.10.1668	Edward Ellison	Willm			Cuthbert Smith	27.12.1679	£2 2 2
18.10.1670	John Smith	John			Cuthbert Smith	28.3.1676	£2 4 3
26.4.1671	John Peirson	Thomas			Cuthbert Smith	18.4.1682	£2 5 5
10.6.1671	William Drauer	Richard			John Beckworth		
3.7.1668	Christopher Grame	James			Leonard Middleton		
3.1.1671	George Humble	John			Thomas Steele	†	
2.1.1673	Cuthbert Hopper	Cuthbert			William Chaitor	*	
10.5.1673	George Viccars	William			Thomas Wrangham sen.	29.9.1685	£2 9 2
5.5.1673	Raiph Morton	John			John Watson		
3.9.1673	Thomas Hinckes	Edward			Edward Greene	*	
18.10.1673	Christopher Fawbridge	Christ.			John Fairebridge	27.12.1680	£2 3 3
7.10.1673	Thomas Carnell	John			Thomas Sporne		
29.12.1673	John Stafford	Roger			George Nicholson	*	

232

Date of indenture	Name of apprentice	Christian name of Father	Occupation of Father	Place of origin	Shipwright to whom apprenticed	Date of freedom	Price for freedom
11.11.1673	William Swinhoe	James			Wm Cooke		
20.10.1673	John Atkinson	Anthony			Thomas Wrangham jun.		
19.5.1674	John Ostins	John			John Watson		
1.5.1674	Thomas Wilson	Thomas			George Nicholson	25.7.1689	
11.4.1674	Francis Dixon	William			Cuthbert Hunter		
11.5.1674	Thomas Fenwicke	Raiph			Thomas Poide		
10.6.1674	John Harle	Thomas			Edward Greene		
3.2.1674	William Lownsdale	Mathew			Thomas Peacock		
29.6.1674	John Gordan	John			Mathew Hutchinson	25.7.1689	
12.8.1674	Robert Forster	Nicholas			Henry Earle		
22.8.1674	Robert Haslipp	Wm			James Bourne		
15.8.1672	Anthony Johnson	Robert			Francis Greene		
13.11.1674	William Hedley	John			Thomas Steele	*	
26.7.1669	Richard Chambers	Oswold			John Wilkinson	27.12.1689	£4 2 2
14.11.1674	William Currey	Robert			William Lawson		
26.12.1674	Thomas Smith	Edward			Leonard Middleton		
10.10.1674	William Reed	Thomas			Thomas Read	27.12.1683	
15.2.1675	Thomas Jopling	Lancelott			Henry Cooke		
2.2.1675	John Atkinson	William			Mathew Read	27.12.1689	
10.2.1675	Ralph Barber	Thomas			Edward Durham		
2.1.1675	Thomas Milbourne	William			Thomas Read		
6.6.1675	William Fletcher	Nicholas	Tailor		John Milbourne	28.12.1685	£2 2 2
18.3.1675	John Wilkinson	Mathew	Yeoman (decd)		Richard Thew	28.12.1685	£2 2 2
20.5.1675	Robert Pearson	John	Yeoman (decd)				
1.6.1675	James Read	James			John Lettany		
					Rowland Kirkley		

Date of indenture	Name of apprentice	Christian name of Father	Occupation of Father	Place of origin	Shipwright to whom apprenticed	Date of freedom	Price for freedom
25.4.1670	Thomas Chilton	Thomas			John Wilkinson		
11.1.1675	Edward Hedley	William			Cuthbert Bone		
30.11.1675	Robert Hutson	John			John Watson		
18.10.1675	John Jackson	Lancelot			Martin Chaitor		
20.12.1675	Richard Forster	George			John Thompson		
3.9.1675	John Hardiman	John			Anthony Wilkinson		
4.1.1676	Lancelott Mills	Mathew			Raiph Thew		
22.1.1676	Christopher Hopper	Christopher			John Luckey		
2.2.1676	Edward Preston	John			John Colier	24.6.1691	£2 10 10
3.2.1676	George Potts	Thomas			George Nicholson		
1.8.1675	James Haistings	George			George Tailor		
21.2.1676	Thomas Finley	Robert			George Taylor		
24.1.1676	Christopher Loansdale	Mathew			Thomas Peacock		
11.2.1676	William Wright	William			John Wright		
3.3.1676	John Pattison	Mathew			Cuthbert Smith		
6.3.1676	William Carr	George			Michaell Wilkinson		
19.2.1676	Robert Lumsdell	Ralph			Michaell Wilkinson		
3.2.1676	Thomas Cooke	Richard			Luke Cooke		
27.3.1676	Ralph Robinson	Michaell			Roger Reay	27.12.1687	£2 7 6
29.3.1676	Michael Elder	John			Mathew Hutchinson		
1.4.1676	George Robinson	Thomas			Mathew Read	1.10.1689	£2 8 8
13.5.1676	Henry Young	William			William Brasier		
11.5.1676	Thomas Parsivall	Richard			Thomas Tailor		
12.9.1676	Thomas Viccars	William			Robert Simpson		
1.4.1676	William Clerk	William			William Hunter		
22.6.1676	Peter Hutchinson	William			Anthony Kirkley		
13.7.1676	Henry Sanderson	Henry			Thomas Foxton		
8.8.1676	Thomas Tulip	Edward			Robert Davison		

Date of indenture	Name of apprentice	Christian name of Father	Occupation of Father	Place of origin	Shipwright to whom apprenticed	Date of freedom	Price for freedom
29.6.1676	Peter Silvertopp	Robert			Richard Thew		
7.6.1676	Henry Bell	Luke			Nicholas Dent	27.12.1683	
19.5.1676	Henry Stobbs	James			John Milbourne		
16.6.1676	Thomas Olliver	Thomas			Cuthbert Bone		
16.5.1676	John Coward	John			William Coward		
16.9.1676	John Robson	Robert			John Armstrong		
25.7.1676	Henry Butterfield	Simon			John Wilkinson	14.4.1691	£2 8 8
31.7.1676	John Downes	William			John Armstrong		
30.3.1675	Michaell Addamson	George			Anthony Wilkinson		
7.11.1673	Raiph Hooke	Raiph			John Beckwith	18.4.1682	£2 2 2
27.5.1676	William Hind	John			Edward Durham	29.9.1687	
1.5.1676	Thomas Turner	Martin			Edward Wilson		
19.10.1676	George Hamleton	John			William Hunter		
25.6.1675	Robert Scaife	John			Francis Greene		
20.10.1675	Ralph Richardson	Robert			Francis Greene		
30.5.1676	Anthony Atkinson	Charles			Thomas Atkinson	1.10.1689	£2 8 8
7.12.1676	Richard Carr	Andrew			George Greene		
19.8.1676	Edward Richmond	Richard			Thomas Wrangham sen.		
24.9.1676	Richard Hopson	Francis			Thomas Wrangham jun.	24.6.1691	£2 5 5
21.8.1676	William Twentyman	John			Thomas Wrangham jun.	25.7.1689	
23.1.1677	John Crossby	William			Ralph Parkin	26.12.1691	£2 10 10
9.2.1677	William Jobling	Lancelott			John Watson		
24.2.1677	John Procter	Robert			Thomas Wrangham sen.	24.6.1692	
28.12.1676	James Unthank	Ralph			John Trewhitt jun.		

Date of indenture	Name of apprentice	Christian name of Father	Occupation of Father	Place of origin	Shipwright to whom apprenticed	Date of freedom	Price for freedom		
19.2.1677	John Hume	John			William Lawson	29.9.1684			
11.3.1677	William Jefferson	John			John Wilkinson				
9.5.1677	Edward Grey	James			Thomas Salkeild	28.12.1685	£2	2	2
21.4.1677	Thomas Nicholson	Anthony			John Earle				
30.4.1677	Richard Urwen	Thomas			George Nicholson	28.12.1690			
5.3.1677	Anthony Fletcher	John			Thomas Poyd				
3.7.1677	William Forster	Peter			His father				
6.6.1677	John Makepeace	Nicholas			Louvaine Rooxby	14.4.1691	£2	7	2
8.6.1677	Joseph Garth	Anthony			Thomas Forster jun.				
1.5.1677	Edward Fargye	Edward			Michael Wilkinson				
27.8.1677	Thomas Strother	Thomas			Thomas Salkeild				
4.10.1677	John Harrison	Richard			Thomas Reed				
19.10.1677	John Crow	John			Cuth. Smith				
10.11.1677	Robert Walton	Antho.			Martin Earle				
4.12.1677	Robert Pattison	George			Roger Fawcus				
1.10.1677	William Belly	Robert			Robert Beckworth	21.12.1691	£2	9	9
[?]	William Hall				Wm Forster	27.12.1677	£2	5	2
23.3.1678	Gilbert Dixon	Thomas			Robert Beckworth	27.12.1690			
2.2.1678	John Haswell	Ralph			John Trewhitt sen.				
4.2.1678	John Cleugh	Robert			Mathew Hutchinson				
2.2.1678	John Dickinson	Robert			Roger Durham				
2.2.1678	Henry James	John			William Chaitor				
2.2.1678	Robert Potts	John			Cuthbert Bone	25.7.1689			
1.4.1678	John Hedlam	Anthony			Nicholas Raine	8.10.1722	£5	5	2
12.1.1678	James Tate	Lionell			William Brasen				
23.3.1678	Cuthbert Hall	William			Edward Greene	22.4.1690	£6	6	8
3.5.1678	Robert Milbourne	John			Cuthbert Smith	29.3.1687	£2	4	2
2.2.1678	Robert Robson	Robert			John Harrison	25.7.1689			

Date of indenture	Name of apprentice	Christian name of Father	Occupation of Father	Place of origin	Shipwright to whom apprenticed	Date of freedom	Price for freedom
5.7.1678	Nathaniell Carnaby	John			Henry Cooke	†	
13.12.1678	William Crosby	William			Ralph Parkin		
5.11.1678	William Wilkinson	Henry			Mathew Read		
21.3.1679	Thomas Heddon	John			John Luckey		
22.4.1679	George Cook	William			His father		
14.1.1679	William Wilkinson	John			Michael Wilkinson	6.4.1686	£2 4 6
1.7.1677	Edward Prockter	Robert			Peter Greene	27.12.1684	
16.5.1679	Samuell Burton	Willm			Robert Davison	25.7.1689	£2 5 5
4.4.1679	Arthur Priscott	George			Jeremiah Cooke	25.6.1688	
1.5.1679	William Douthwaite	Thomas			John Thompson		
24.4.1679	Thomas Read	Edward			Edward Allison		
1.5.1679	John Harrison	John			William Parke		
10.5.1679	Peter Farmer	Cuthbert			Thomas Robinson	1.10.1689	£2 6 6
1.5.1679	Ralph Commin	Simon			Henry Cooke	25.7.1689	
4.6.1679	Thomas Dixon	John			Henry Earle	21.12.1691	£2 7 7
24.6.1679	Stephen Jolly	Thomas			John Unthank	27.12.1689	
26.7.1679	John Fewler	Peter			Thomas Foxton	25.7.1689	
27.12.1679	John Elsdon	Ralph			His father		
30.4.1677	George Wilson	James			Rowland Kirkley	25.7.1689	
21.1.1678	Mark Bell	Henry			Rowland Kirkley	28.12.1685	£2 2 2
20.2.1680	Anthony Nicholson	William			John Beckwith		
5.3.1680	Nicholas Sailes	Nicholas			Edward Allison		
20.10.1680	Lancelott Goodson	Richard			John Goodson	25.7.1689	
20.10.1675	Ralph Richardson	Robert	Yeoman	Benwilch	Francis Green		
30.2.1675	Archbald Coxon	Ralph	Yeoman	Reedwater	Richard Wallas	4.10.1686	£2 4 6
10.9.1675	Joseph Huntridge	Samuell	Gent (decd)	Glanton	Richard Wallas		
5.11.1681	George Charlton	John	(decd)	Coldtowne	Richard Wallas		

237

Date of indenture	Name of apprentice	Christian name of Father	Occupation of Father	Place of origin	Shipwright to whom apprenticed	Date of freedom	Price for freedom
14.8.1676	Robert Skaife	John	Yeoman	Heighington, Durham	Tho. Poide	27.12.1684	
31.8.1681	Henry Burnes	William	Yeoman	Blaidon, Durham	Thomas Poyd		
3.8.1682	George Young	John	Yeoman	Doding	Thomas Barber		£6 17 4
9.2.1683	Joseph Forster	Edward	Yeoman	Whitstonehouse	Thomas Reed	27.12.1694	
[?]	Walter Trumble	George	Yeoman	Newcastle	John Beckwith	29.9.1687	
7.9.1683	William Carlisle	Herbert	Gent	Cumberland	Jerem. Cook		
[?]	George Wilson	Wm		Hadston	Edward Green	27.12.1690	
5.3.1681	Thomas Cooper	Tho.	Yeoman	Newcastle	Cuthbert Bone		
2.4.1684	Ralph Heslopp	Patrick	Yeoman	Newcastle	John Collyer		
19.4.1684	Wm Hall	John	Yeoman	Newcastle	Jeremiah Cook	28.12.1691	£2 4 10
1.6.1684	Mathew Hedley	Robert		Elsdon	Thomas Wrangham		
22.7.1684	Matthew Alder	Henry	Yeoman	Alenham	Henry Cook		
11.11.1684	Thomas Newton	Henry		Hadley-in-the-Hill	Edward Ellison	29.9.1693	£2 4 4
1.2.1684	Ralph Thew	John	Yeoman	Swinhoe	Robert Silvertopp		
1.4.1685	William Smith	William	Yeoman (decd)				
8.5.1685	Mathew Burtch	George	Yeoman	Togstone	Thomas Barber		
19.3.1685	Thomas Bailes	William	Yeoman	Newcastle	George Nicholson		
1.8.1684	Thomas Gillery	John	Gent	Hunderthwaite, Yorks.	Edward Greene		
30.5.1685	James Noton	John	Yeoman	Lumley Park, Durham	Christopher Gillery		
2.2.1685	Robert Carr	William	Yeoman (decd)	Newcastle	Rowland Kirkley		
30.9.1685	Ralph Andrew	Ralph	Yeoman	Woodhall Greencroft, Durham	Thomas Wrangham Robert Beckwith		

Date of indenture	Name of apprentice	Christian name of Father	Occupation of Father	Place of origin	Shipwright to whom apprenticed	Date of freedom	Price for freedom
7.7.1686	George Farrow	Thomas	Weaver (decd)	Scremerstone, Durham	[?]		
26.3.1686	Edward Slater	Edward	Shipwright (decd)				
25.3.1686	George Emerson	Ralph	Shipwright	Newcastle	Thomas Reed	27.12.1694	£2 4 4
10.6.1686	Cuthbert Charlton	John	Yeoman	Newcastle	Thomas Poyde	27.12.1693	£2 4 4
26.4.1686	Thomas Orange	William	Turner	Coldtowne	Richard Wallas		
1.5.1686	Christopher Parker	Robert	Yeoman	Edlingham	Edward Ellison	29.9.1694	£2 4 4
[?]	Frank Mayers	Thomas	Yeoman	Carlisle	John Colyer	29.3.1687	£2 3 3
10.2.1687	William Trumble	Cuthbert	Yeoman	Hetton Henry, Durham	Cuthbert Hopper	27.12.1694	£2 6 6
18.10.1686	George Blyth	James	Maltster	Newcastle	Thomas Barber		
2.5.1687	Thomas Liddle	James	Gent	Newcastle	Edward Ellison	27.12.1695	£2 2 2
16.4.1680	William Spence	James	Saltmaker	Teem Staith, Durham	Anthony Wilkinson		
11.7.1682	Wm Watson	John	Yeoman	Southsheilds, Durham	Anthony Wilkinson		
18.5.1687	Thomas Forster	John		Sherton, Durham	Jeremiah Cooke	27.12.1695	£2 3 3
13.5.1687	Jonathan Nicholson	William	Yeoman	Hedworth, Durham	Mathew Hutchinson		
6.5.1687	John Young	John	Yeoman	Cudderstone, Yorks.	Edward Greene		
12.12.1687	Ralph Oastons	John	Yeoman	Newcastle	Christopher Gilery		
2.4.1689	William Briseau	John	Yeoman (decd)	Fleetham	John Collyer	24.6.1698	£2 2 2
27.7.1689	Thomas Chatt	Thomas	Yeoman	Ovington Northumberland	John Collyer		
9.8.1689	George Snawball	John	Yeoman	Newbrough	Rowland Kirkley	27.12.1697	£2 3 3
29.1.1685	Michall Sabourne	Tho.		Munckseton	George Snawball John Harle		

239

Date of indenture	Name of apprentice	Christian name of Father	Occupation of Father	Place of origin	Shipwright to whom apprenticed	Date of freedom	Price for freedom
22.4.1690	Thomas Wilkinson	John		Sandgate, Newcastle	His father		
20.2.1690	Lancelott Burrell	John	Yeoman (decd)				
25.3.1690	Marke Watson	Cuthbert	Yeoman	Widdington Park Coopen	John Wilkinson		
27.6.1688	William Hanby	Francis	Gent	City of Durham	Thomas Poyd		
7.1.1689	John Trumble	John	Yeoman (decd)	Beamish, Durham	Robt Beckworth	24.6.1696	£2 4 4
3.2.1688	John Reed	Edward	Yeoman	The Cragg	Robt Beckworth	27.12.1698	£2 6 6
10.2.1690	James Dixon	Lyonell	Yeoman	Thruple	Thom. Reed		
13.6.1690	John Younghusband	Wm	Yeoman (decd)		Thom. Reed		
3.4.1690	Henry Cay	John	Marriner	Budell	Rowland Kirkley	26.4.1698	£2 4 4
14.6.1690	John Nixon	John	Yeoman	Newcastle	Thomas Wailes	24.6.1698	£2 2 2
25.11.1690	Christopher Hewitson	Wm	Yeoman	Buddell	Richard Wallas		
2.2.1682	William Pearson	Anthony (decd)		Harton, Durham	Richard Coates		
28.2.1690	Stephen Morres			Southshields, Durham	John Wilkinson		
15.5.1689	John Russell	Simon	Yeoman	Layton, Durham	John Wilkinson		
12.2.1691	Francis White	George	Yeoman	Walworth, Durham	John Wilkinson		
6.3.1691	William Younghusband	Edward	Weaver	Budell	Jeremiah Cooke	29.12.1700	
13.4.1691	John Sanderson	Michaell	Yeoman	Beale of the Hill, Durham	Thomas Barber		
6.3.1691	Richard Hudson	Richard	Yeoman	Tinemouth	Mark Bell / Thomas Hudson	11.4.1721	£4 10 6
21.3.1691	John Dickon	John	Yeoman	Houghton, Durham	Marmaduke Smithson		

Date of indenture	Name of apprentice	Christian name of Father	Occupation of Father	Place of origin	Shipwright to whom apprenticed	Date of freedom	Price for freedom
1.6.1691	George Trumble	Thomas	Yeoman	Kirk Newton	Thomas Trumble		
2.6.1691	John Gillary	John	Yeoman	Whickham, Durham			
[?].1691	George Todd	Robt			John Pearson		
[?].1691	John Potter	Wm			His father	*	
1.8.1689	Thomas Mathewson	John	Yeoman	Spindleston	His father		
1.8.1690	Zachariah Brand	John	Yeoman	Newcastle	Henry Wrangham	27.12.1701	
16.6.1690	James Wilson	James	Yeoman	Newcastle	Henry Wrangham	27.12.1699	£2 3 0
11.7.1691	Robert Richardson	Robert	Yeoman	Newcastle	George Wilson	27.12.1699	£2 2 0
28.12.1691	Thomas Storey	Thomas			Thomas Campion		
28.12.1691	George Storey	Thomas			His father	26.4.1698	£2 2 2
28.12.1691	John Storey	Thomas			His father	30.3.1703	£2 2 2
12.10.1691	Samuell Tulipp	George	Yeoman	Cowpen	Thomas Poide	29.9.1699	£2 2 0
15.8.1691	Leonard Wilson	John	Yeoman	Cotherston, Yorks.	Mathew Hutchinson		
7.10.1691	Peter Waite	John	Marriner (decd)	Newcastle	Marmaduke Smithson	29.9.1699	£2 3 0
1.10.1691	Ralph Reed	Edward	Yeoman	The Crage	Thomas Reed	27.12.1698	£2 4 4
3.10.1691	George Porter	Charles	Yeoman (decd)	Satwellside, Durham	William Wilkinson	27.12.1701	
8.1.1692	Robert Edger	John	Yeoman	Shordswood	Thomas Campion	27.12.1701	£2 2 2
5.3.1692	John Corby	John	Yeoman	Spen, Durham	Edwd Procter	27.12.1699	
16.4.1692	Henry Purvis	Ralph	Yeoman	East Harford	Edwd Procter	27.12.1699	
29.9.1692	George Comin	Ralph	Yeoman		His father	27.12.1714	£2 2 8
16.1.1692	Robert Collingwood	Robert	Yeoman	Bird Moore, Durham	William Reed	22.4.1701	£2 2 2
15.8.1692	William Milbourne	Roger	Yeoman (decd)	East Dissington	William Twentyman		

Date of indenture	Name of apprentice	Christian name of Father	Occupation of Father	Place of origin	Shipwright to whom apprenticed	Date of freedom	Price for freedom
15.10.1692	John Rutlish	John	Yeoman	Fenham	Edward Blunt		
12.12.1692	John Moore	Edward	Yeoman	Warke	Gawin Robinson		
11.11.1692	Martin Hewes	William	Yeoman	Durham	Edward Allison		
26.12.1692	George Hall	William	Yeoman (decd)				
31.12.1692	George Kitchin	George	Gent (decd)	Sharpton	Roger Durham	27.12.1707	£2 11 11
6.1.1693	John Harrison	Thomas	Yeoman	Long Benton	Edward Preston	4.2.1711	£2 2 2
28.12.1692	Cuthbert Swinbourne	Thomas	Yeoman	Whickham	John Taylor		
15.10.1692	John Simpson	Mungoe		Kenton	Wm Belley	3.4.1711	£2 2 2
29.12.1692	Wm Young	Mathew		Fenham	Edward Blunt		
2.6.1693	Thomas Halliday	George	Yeoman	Sunderland	Thomas Wilson	22.4.1701	£2 2 2
1.5.1693	James Mow	Ralph	Yeoman	Grindon, Durham	Wm Strother		
1.5.1693	Robt Newton	Henry	Yeoman	Sturton Graing	John Gordon		
22.5.1693	Thomas Olliver	Andrew	Yeoman	Hedley	Edward Ellison		
20.7.1692	Robert Earle	Robert	Marriner	Ray	John Thompson		
15.6.1693	Paull Halliday	Henry	Yeoman	Gateshead	Thomas Barber		
8.4.1693	Thomas Anderson	Gerrard	Yeoman	Barnestone, Durham	John Thompson	29.9.1704	£2 7 7
14.8.1693	Nicholas Chapman	Thomas	Yeoman	Northshields	Thomas Poyde		
2.2.1693	Richard Elliott	Richard	Gent (decd)	Norton, Durham	Thomas Campion	*	
26.6.1693	George Maughline	Wm	Yeoman	Hexham	Roger Durham	2.4.1701	£2 2 2
3.7.1693	Mathew George	Mathew	Yeoman (decd)	Newcastle	Edwd Preston		
18.7.1693	Richard Browne	George	Yeoman	Newcastle	Wm Cooke		
1.8.1693	Arthur Liddell	James	Gent	Team Staithe, Durham	Henry Browne	27.12.1701	
1.8.1693	George Grame	James	Yeoman	Newcastle	John Taylor John Procter		

Date of indenture	Name of apprentice	Christian name of Father	Occupation of Father	Place of origin	Shipwright to whom apprenticed	Date of freedom	Price for freedom
18.8.1693	Robert Russell	Nicholas	Yeoman	Netherton, Durham	John Procter		
2.9.1693	John Nelson	Peter	Gent	City of Durham	Edwd Procter	29.9.1707	
26.9.1693	Francis Tubby	Francis	Marriner		Robert Walton		
22.7.1693	John Fenwicke	Thomas	Yeoman	Hedon-on-the-Wall	Thomas Fenwick		
1.11.1693	George Wilkinson	Edward	Yeoman	Middlefield House, Durham	Mathew Hutchinson		
10.8.1693	Thomas Layburne	John	Yeoman (decd)		Thomas Reed	27.12.1701	
28.10.1693	John Browell	John	Yeoman	Causey, Durham	Richard Coates		
24.2.1694	Alex. Swinburne	Samuell	Yeoman	Hedley on the Hill Newcastle	Roger Durham		
20.2.1694	George Iley	George	Yeoman	Killerby, Durham	Marmaduke Smithson		
9.4.1694	Christopher Stephen	James	Yeoman	Newcastle	George Browne	*	
9.4.1694	Wm Sadler	John	Yeoman	Denton Staithe	John Beckwith		
1.5.1694	William Bates	William	Gent	Raby, Durham	Edwd Ellison		
1.5.1694	Alexander Stokoe	Richd	Yeoman	Plender Heath	George Snowball	22.6.1702	
9.5.1694	William Bolam	William	Yeoman	Warne	Thomas Fenwick	27.12.1703	
1.5.1694	Edwd Simpson	Edwd	Marriner	South Shoare, Durham	Edward Blunt		
22.5.1694	Joseph Coward	Wm	Yeoman	Glasshouses	John Goodison		
16.6.1694	Samuell Forster	Robt	Yeoman	Winlington Mill, Durham	George Forster	27.12.1701	
1.8.1694	Samuell Marshall	Thomas	Yeoman (decd)	Wallis Wall	John Smith	27.12.1703	

243

Date of indenture	Name of apprentice	Christian name of Father	Occupation of Father	Place of origin	Shipwright to whom apprenticed	Date of freedom	Price for freedom
4.8.1694	Edward Stobbert	Willm	Yeoman (decd)	Ryton Woodside, Durham	Richard Coates		
26.6.1694	Thomas Drydon	George	Yeoman	Humbleton	Robert Beckwith	30.3.1703	£2 2 2
14.8.1694	John Goodson	Thomas	Yeoman (decd)	Sumerhouse, Durham	John Goodson		
25.1.1694	John Swan	Richard	Yeoman	Bambrough	Arthur Preston		
9.7.1694	Joseph Gladstone	William	Yeoman	Deanhouse	Wm Strother	11.1.1706	£5 8 6
24.4.1694	John Grey	Wm	Yeoman	Bedlington, Durham	John Wilkinson	18.4.1704	£2 2 2
6.11.1694	Robert Jackson	Nicholas	Yeoman	Reedheugh	Edwd Hedley	27.12.1703	
22.12.1694	Thomas Urwen	Richard			His father	*	
1.10.1694	Ambrose Appleby	Ambrose	Yeoman	Cutherston, Yorks.	John Gordon		
1.10.1694	Tho. Keidyea	Wm	Yeoman	Chillingham	John Atkinson		
2.4.1694	Richard Younghusband	Oswald	House-carpenter	Newcastle	Edward Grey	24.6.1703	£2 6 5
7.1.1695	Thomas Scott	James	Yeoman	Newcastle	Thomas Wrangham	30.3.1703	£2 2 2
1.5.1695	William Ward	Ralph	Yeoman	Netherton, Durham	Gilbt Dixon		
1.5.1695	Thomas Thompson	John	Potter	South Shoare, Durham	John Taylor	25.6.1705	£2 2 2
27.6.1695	George Barkas	Nicholas	Yeoman	Snaws Green, Durham	Robt Beckworth		
15.3.1695	Roger Moffitt	Wm	Yeoman	Ovingham	Wm Belly		
15.7.1695	Wm Black	Wm	Marriner	City of London	Thomas Wailes		

Date of indenture	Name of apprentice	Christian name of Father	Occupation of Father	Place of origin	Shipwright to whom apprenticed	Date of freedom	Price for freedom
1.10.1695	Richard Wilson	George	Yeoman	Shotley Bridge, Durham	Robert Beckwith	10.4.1705	£2 2 2
11.11.1695	John Sanderson	John	Yeoman	Plumpton Wall, Cumberland	Jeremiah Cooke		
1.1.1696	William Forster	George	Butcher	Barwick upon Tweed	Wm Strother		
21.1.1696	Thomas Forster	Thomas	Mason	Byker	Wm Twentyman	29.9.1704	£2 5 5
3.3.1696	Thomas Mirriman	Thomas	Gent (decd)	Jarrow, Durham	John Wallas	18.4.1704	£2 2 2
8.6.1696	Ralph Emerson	Ralph	Yeoman	Newcastle	Edward Slaitor		
23.3.1696	William Swinburne	Thomas	Yeoman	Fenham	Stephen Brewhouse		
21.8.1696	Willm Maughlin	Wm	Yeoman	Newcastle	Ralph Wilson	24.6.1704	£2 4 4
8.8.1696	John Ingledue	Thomas	Yeoman	Felling, Durham	John Trewhitt	27.12.1705	£2 5 5
6.5.1697	John Cooke	Thomas	Smith	South Shields, Durham	John Bone		
9.7.1697	Robert Elphington	Thomas	Millwright	Whickham, Durham	John Bone		
2.3.1698	William Reynoldson	William	Yeoman	Choppell, Durham			
19.4.1698	George Hymers	Ralph	Gent (decd)	Stella, Durham	Mathew Hutchinson	29.9.1705	£2 4 4
21.5.1698	Edward Bailes	Edward	Yeoman	South Shields, Durham	Thomas Hutson	27.12.1705	£2 4 4
6.1.1698	Thomas Potts	Robert	(decd)	Hedworth, Durham	Edwd Potts	*	
1.8.1698	Jeremiah Milbourne	Cuthbert	Gent	Newcastle	Edwd Wilkinson	2.4.1706	£2 4 4
16.6.1698	John Reed	Edward	Yeoman	Great Whittington	Mark Bell	27.12.1706	£2 5 5
18.11.1698	John Roper	Richard	Waterman	North Shields	Tho. Reed / Thomas Wilkinson		
2.2.1699	Cuthbert Watson	Henry	Yeoman	Gateshead	Arthur Prescodd	3.4.1706	£2 4 4

Date of indenture	Name of apprentice	Christian name of Father	Occupation of Father	Place of origin	Shipwright to whom apprenticed	Date of freedom	Price for freedom
12.5.1699	Robert Read	Ralph	Yeoman (decd)	Coldtowne, Ridsdale	Wm Read		
1.5.1699	John Duck	John	Yeoman	Hessell, Kingston-upon-Hull, Yorks.			
11.1.1698	Thomas Browne	John	Shipwright (decd)	South Shields, Durham	William Hall		
3.7.1699	Robert Akenside	William	Gent (decd)		Thomas Campion		
1.1.1700	Thomas Waugh	John	Marriner	Hawkwell	Richard Wallas	15.4.1707	£2 4 4
14.2.1700	Robert Grey	John	(decd)	Newcastle	Peter Waite		
1.5.1700	George Ferrer	Wm	Keelman	Newcastle	Thomas Poyd		
17.8.1700	Oswold Carnes	Cuthbert	Yeoman	Gt Lawrence, Glasshouses Forthhouse	Thomas Wallas	29.9.1712	£2 8 8
11.11.1700	Thomas Gally	John	Yeoman		Thomas Campion	2.2.1708	£2 4 4
4.1.1701	Thomas Shotten	Thomas	Marriner (decd)	Gateshead	Edward Blunt	27.12.1707	£2 2 2
14.8.1701	Charles Reay	Robert	Yeoman (decd)	Newcastle	Thomas Liddle		
7.3.1701	Giles Gallon	William	House-carpenter	Newcastle	Richard Coates		
1.1.1702	Samuel Wake	Thomas	Yeoman (decd)	Hallistowe	Edwd Blunt	29.9.1708	£2 4 4
1.1.1702	Ralph Soulsby	Robert	Gent	Gateshead	Mark Bell	21.12.1709	£2 4 4
14.11.1702	John Harrison	Wm	Gent	Camboe	Thomas Liddle	30.7.1713	£2 2 2
30.11.1702	Wm Anderson	Wm	Yeoman	Winnowe Lee	Wm Reed	3.4.1711	£2 5 4
			Baker & Brewer (decd)	Newcastle	Thomas Wrangham		

246

Date of indenture	Name of apprentice	Christian name of Father	Occupation of Father	Place of origin	Shipwright to whom apprenticed	Date of freedom	Price for freedom
13.10.1702	Isaac Cooper	Isaac	Master Marriner	South Shields	Wm Wrangham		
3.2.1703	Thomas Smith	Robert	Yeoman	Alnwick	Robt Walton		
15.3.1703	Wm Stole	Wm	Marriner	Dents Hole	Thomas Wrangham		
12.2.1703	Richard Stokoe	Richard	Yeoman	Newbrough	Thomas Campion		
26.3.1703	Wm Drydon	Geo.	Yeoman	Humbleston	Thomas Wrangham		
17.4.1703	Charles Emerson	James	Yeoman	Dunston, Durham	Mark Bell	2.10.1710	£2 10 2
31.3.1703	Wm Fletcher	Wm	Butcher	Newcastle	Marmaduke Smithson	31.3.1712	£2 5 5
7.4.1703	Henry Stainsby	John	Yeoman	Langley Park, Durham	Jeremiah Cooke	27.12.1712	£2 6 6
1.4.1703	John Saburne	John	Yeoman	Chirton	Thomas Wallas	3.4.1716	£3 6 2
5.10.1703	Peter Lambert	Jonathan	Gent (decd)	Newcastle	Peter Waite	22.8.1711	£2 5 4
29.9.1703	Joseph Errington	Joseph	Butcher	Newcastle	Robert Kirkley		
5.1.1703	George Slaiter	Eliah	Marriner (decd)		John Bone		
1.1.1704	John Rotherford	John	Yeoman	Newcastle	Thomas Campion	27.12.1712	£2 2 2
1.1.1704	Henry Harrison	Wm	Yeoman	Walker	John Trewhitt	27.12.1712	£2 6 10
29.12.1703	Wm Carr	Wm	Yeoman	Cramlington	Thomas Reed sen.	21.4.1712	£2 2 2
29.12.1703	Wm Wilson	Wm	Yeoman	Craigin	Thomas Reed jun.	29.9.1711	£4 2 2
2.2.1704	Thomas Shaftoe	Arthur	Anchor Smith	Newcastle	Thomas Reed jun.	29.9.1711	£2 6 10
2.2.1704	Thomas Dixon	Robert	Yeoman	Hartley	Gilbert Dixon	24.6.1714	£2 7 10
17.4.1704	Thomas Maughlin	Wm	Yeoman	Newcastle	Peter Waite	7.5.1714	
2.7.1704	Radcliffe Fowler	Richard	Yeoman	Rothbury	Thomas Wrangham		
24.4.1704	Thomas Trumble	Wm	Yeoman	Westwoodburne	Thomas Reed		
3.8.1704	Joseph Heaton	Thomas	Yeoman	Newcastle	Thomas Wilkinson	27.3.1712	
8.6.1704	George Carr	Alex.	Merchant	Berwicke upon Tweed	Edward Slater		

Date of indenture	Name of apprentice	Christian name of Father	Occupation of Father	Place of origin	Shipwright to whom apprenticed	Date of freedom	Price for freedom
10.10.1704	Ralph Reed	Clement	Yeoman	Cold Towne	Wm Reed	7.4.1713	£2 7 11
27.11.1704	Brian Wall	Brian	Marriner	Newcastle	Geo. Forster	22.8.1711	£2 6 10
22.12.1704	Thomas Midleird	Archbald	Fisherman	Hartley	Gilbert Dixon		
1.1.1704	Ralph Stell	Ralph	Yeoman	South Shoare, Durham			
6.4.1705	Thomas Potts	Thomas	Cooper	Newcastle	Richard Wallas	29.9.1711	£2 8 4
5.5.1705	Joseph Charlton	Wm	Yeoman	Kenton	Wm Strother	26.12.1713	£2 12 8
1.6.1705	Robert Atkinson	Wm		Monkseaton	Henry Purvis		
2.7.1705	William Brownrigg	Wm	Yeoman	City of Durham	Thomas Liddle		
25.8.1705	Robert Coulson	Wm	Yeoman	Durham	Edwd Blunt		
24.6.1705	Robert Glenton	Jeffery	Yeoman	Low Consley, Durham	Peter Waite	7.4.1713	£2 5 4
1.6.1705	John Shinon	Thomas	Yeoman	Gateshead	Wm Wrangham	17.4.1713	£2 5 10
23.10.1705	John Wheatley	Robert	Wheelwright	Tamesbrigs, Durham	Thomas Reed jun.		
18.10.1705	Benjamin Butyman	Wm	Shipwright	Newcastle	Thomas Reed jun.	27.12.1714	£2 6 5
2.10.1705	Thomas Pattison	Robt	Yeoman	Parkhouse, Durham	John Butiman		
26.1.1706	Zachariah Hull	Richard	Yeoman (decd)	Ferside, Durham	Richd Wallas	29.9.1713	£2 6 10
20.10.1705	Patrick Sudis	Thomas	Yeoman	Teembridge, Durham	John Beckwith	8.6.1714	£2 6 5
7.1.1706	Geo. Maughlin	Wm	Shipwright	Newcastle	Thomas Wrangham	29.9.1713	£2 5 4
11.3.1706	Mathew Graham	James	Yeoman	Newcastle	George Maughlin		
11.2.1706	William Staward	Robert	Yeoman	St Anthonies	Roger Durham	27.12.1715	£3 0 11
7.1.1706	Thomas Lattimore	Wm	Yeoman	Ousburne	Jeremiah Cook	24.6.1713	£2 5 4
26.1.1706	George Aubovey	John	Yeoman	South Shoare, Durham	Wm Wrangham		
					Thomas Wallas		

Date of indenture	Name of apprentice	Christian name of Father	Occupation of Father	Place of origin	Shipwright to whom apprenticed	Date of freedom	Price for freedom
20.4.1706	John Thowborne	Thomas	Yeoman (decd)	Newcastle	James Lowson	27.12.1714	£2 6 4
17.6.1706	Cuthbert Lee	John	Yeoman (decd)	West Yeckham	Wm Strother	21.12.1715	£4 19 11
6.6.1706	Tho. Bell	Wm	Anchor Smith	Newcastle	Tho. Barber		
30.11.1706	Cuthbert Dickinson	Thomas	Yeoman	Shotley Bridge, Durham			
2.12.1706	Robert Guy	John	Yeoman	Gateshead	Wm Strother	27.12.1714	£2 6 5
1.7.1706	Thomas Donkin	Robert		Old Bewicke	Ralph Reed	24.6.1714	£2 2 2
16.7.1706	Thomas Turner	John	Marriner	Newcastle	Arthur Liddle		
5.5.1707	James Thompson	John	Yeoman	Newcastle	Zachariah Brand		
1.5.1707	Robert Bradley	George	Baker (decd)	North Shields	John Backworth	19.4.1715	£2 11 10
2.8.1707	Joseph Campion	Robert		Mask in Cleaveland, Yorks.	Thomas Wallas	27.12.1714	£2 5 10
12.11.1707	Wm Lidster	Richard	Yeoman	Coxgreen, Durham	Thomas Campion	27.12.1714	£2 4 10
9.3.1708	James White	Enoch	Weaver	Bishop Auckland, Durham	Paul Holliday		
20.5.1708	John Hewison	John	Yeoman	Newcastle	Edward Blunt	6.1.1718	£3 16 6
1.5.1708	John Charlton	William	Yeoman	Henson	Roger Durham jun.	22.12.1715	£2 12 4
20.9.1708	Ralph Bolam	William	Yeoman	Easington Grainge	William Trewhitt	27.12.1715	£5 12 10
20.9.1708	Archbald Graham	James	Marriner	Newcastle	William Bolam		
27.12.1708	Richard Swann	Edward	Marriner	Newcastle	Cuthbert Watson		
27.9.1708	George Collinson	Israel	Gent	Newcastle	John Goodson	25.6.1716	£2 13 4
[?].2.1700	Wm Trumble	Wm		Woodburne	John Beckwith	27.12.1708	£2 4 4
4.10.1708	Robert Atkinson	Thomas	Skinner	Newcastle	Thomas Reed Thomas Lidle	27.12.1716	£2 16 10

Date of indenture	Name of apprentice	Christian name of Father	Occupation of Father	Place of origin	Shipwright to whom apprenticed	Date of freedom	Price for freedom
1.5.1709	George Tulip	John	Yeoman	Whitteridge	Tho. Wallas		
17.11.1709	George Carr	Thomas	Yeoman	Huton, Scotland	Edward Slater	*	
2.3.1709	John Parker	Job	Merchant	Newcastle	Jeremiah Cook		
10.1.1710	Thomas Lushey			Simonsfield, Durham			
17.5.1710	Joseph Harle	Thomas	Yeoman	Hexham	Edwd Wilkinson	27.12.1717	£4 9 4
17.6.1710	Robert Huntley	John	Gent	Sunderland	Paul Halliday		
20.3.1710	John Shipherd	Henry	Yeoman (decd)	Sunderland	Paul Halliday		
5.7.1710	Thomas Ridley	Thomas	Yeoman	Newsham	Thomas Wallas	27.12.1718	£3 2 9
16.3.1711	Michaell Dawson	Mathew	Cordwainer	Tencklanes, Durham	William Wrangham	14.4.1718	£2 11 3
8.12.1710	Gilbert Lermouth	Tho.		Newcastle	Tho. Campion	24.6.1718	£2 5 9
13.4.1710	Edward Robson	Wm	Yeoman	Greens	Richd Wallas		
9.6.1711	Thomas Baird	Thomas	Yeoman	Bellingham	Ralph Reed	29.6.1718	£2 16 10
11.6.1711	John Reed	James	Shipwright	Gateshead	Thomas Reed jun.	31.3.1719	£4 12 4
4.9.1711	John Rowen	Andrew	Yeoman	Sunderland	Thomas Reed jun.		
2.2.1710	James Fletcher	Christopher		Newcastle	Peter Waite	*	
28.2.1712	Wm Henderson	Geo.	Yeoman	Gateshead	Edward Blunt	27.12.1718	£2 9 8
1.1.1712	Geo. Brown	John	Yeoman	Newcastle	Peter Waite	18.10.1720	£2 7 10
12.7.1712	Stephen Watson	Antho.	Yeoman	Earsdon	Jeremiah Cook	*	
13.10.1712	Jonathan French	Jonath.	Smith	Bainbridgehouse, Durham	Thos Reed, jun.	6.1.1720	£2 4 4
3.2.1713	Anthony Trumble	Wm	Yeoman	Newcastle	Peter Waite	24.6.1721	£2 4 4
4.5.1713	Andrew Hay	Walter	Keelman	West Woodburn	Jeremiah Cooke	9.12.1720	£2 4 4
20.5.1713	John Simple	John	Yeoman	Newcastle	Roger Durham jun.	9.12.1720	£2 4 4
4.5.1713	John Charleton	Cuthbert	Shipwright (decd)	Newcastle	John Beckwith		
				North Sheilds	George Taylor	9.12.1720	£2 4 4

Date of indenture	Name of apprentice	Christian name of Father	Occupation of Father	Place of origin	Shipwright to whom apprenticed	Date of freedom	Price for freedom		
11.6.1713	Thomas Williamson	Thos.	Yeoman (decd)	Gateshead	Richard Wallas	24.6.1721	£2	5	4
13.6.1713	Wm Hay	Alexander	Yeoman	Newcastle	John Goodson	27.12.1720	£2	4	10
3.7.1713	Abraham Dowson	Thomas	Yeoman (decd)	Gateshead	Thomas Reed sen.	27.12.1720	£2	5	4
31.12.1713	Henry Ovington	Henry	Yeoman	Newcastle	Robert Richardson	25.1.1722	£2	6	5
16.1.1714	John Crisp	John	Yeoman	Feildhouse, Durham	Wm Reed	27.3.1722	£2	5	10
2.2.1714	John Bateson	Richard	Yeoman	Ewsburn	Thomas Campion	*			
25.3.1714	Christopher Dawson	Thomas	Yeoman (decd)	Newbrough	Geo. Snowball	27.12.1722	£2	4	4
29.3.1714	Jos. Thompson	John	Yeoman (decd)	Newcastle	John Trewhitt	27.3.1722	£2	4	4
1.1.1714	Robert Pinn	Robert	Yeoman	Wells, Norfolk	Edward Slater				
1.5.1714	Matthew Nicholson	Geo.	Yeoman	Brunton	Thomas Wrangham	27.3.1722			
22.6.1714	Benjamin Thompson	John	Yeoman (decd)	Newcastle	John Beckwith	*			
5.4.1714	Richard Bennett	Richard	Yeoman	Swalwell, Durham	James Wallas				
5.4.1714	John Carier	Arthur	Gent	City of Durham	Thomas Wallas	27.3.1722	£2	8	4
13.4.1714	Mark Milburn	Cuthbert	Yeoman (decd)	Newcastle	Jeremiah Milburn	18.9.1722	£2	5	5
8.9.1714	Thomas Harrison	Michael	Yeoman	Newcastle	Peter Forster	16.4.1723	£2	6	10
10.4.1714	Francis Hull	John	Yeoman	Ousterly, Durham	Jeremiah Cook	*			
7.7.1714	George Muris	John	Yeoman	Newcastle	Richard Younghusband	21.12.1724	£2	6	6
6.8.1714	Thomas Inglish [English]	Robert	Yeoman	Benwell	Roger Durham	30.3.1722	£2	5	4

Date of indenture	Name of apprentice	Christian name of Father	Occupation of Father	Place of origin	Shipwright to whom apprenticed	Date of freedom	Price for freedom
13.7.1714	Antho. Perryman	Wm	Yeoman (decd)	Newcastle	Wm Park		
3.2.1715	Benjamin Bailes	John	Yeoman	Dents Hole	John Goodson	29.9.1722	£2 5 4
4.5.1715	Cuthbert Means	James	Yeoman	Newcastle	John Beckwith	27.12.1723	£2 4 10
2.5.1715	John Mow [More]	John	Yeoman	Newcastle	Wm Fletcher jun.		
6.5.1715	Andrew Hagston	Charles	Yeoman (decd)	Newcastle	Wm Fletcher jun.	7.4.1724	£2 4 4
16.2.1715	Thomas Shepherd	Henry	Yeoman	Seaton Delavall	Gilbert Dixon	28.12.1724	£2 8 4
1.7.1715	Cuthbert Watson	Henry	Yeoman (decd)	Gateshead	Roger Durham	27.12.1725	£2 18 0
17.8.1715	Cha. Lucas	Gilbert	Yeoman	Newcastle	Wm Reed	30.9.1723	£2 4 4
1.10.1715	Ralph Pratt	John	Yeoman	Newcastle	Peter Forster	24.6.1723	£4 4 4
31.3.1715	Henry Clarke	James	Yeoman	Bedlington, Durham	Jeremiah Cooke		
7.11.1715	Robert Blakelock	William	Waller	South Sheilds, Durham	Thomas Shaftoe	20.9.1722	£4 2 4
[?]	John Trumble	John	Yeoman		Thomas Reed sen.	27.12.1715	£2 14 4
22.2.1716	John Tulipp	Cuthbert	Shipwright	Cowpen	Samuel Tulipp	30.9.1723	£2 4 4
5.4.1716	Jonathan Charleton	John	Cooper	Northsheilds	William Turnbull	30.9.1723	£2 4 4
1.5.1716	Robert Storey	Samuel	Yeoman	Northsheilds	James Lowson		
1.5.1716	John Pye	Peter	Yeoman	South Sheilds	James Lowson		
5.6.1716	Thomas Chandler	Joseph	Yeoman	Newcastle	Roger Durham		
25.6.1716	Edward Barrowfoot	Robert	Yeoman	Berick, Durham	James Wilson		
26.6.1716	Edward Read	Charles	Joyner	Northumberland	Thomas Read sen.		
17.8.1716	Charles Stockell	Wm	Plumber	North Sheilds	Averah Trewhitt		
1.7.1716	Edward Preston			Newcastle	Cuthbert Preston	8.8.1723	£2 4 4
12.11.1716	William Reed	Ralph	Yeoman	Picktree, Durham	Thomas Wallas	*	
26.11.1716	William Tindall	William	Glassmaker	Newcastle	James Wallas	4.12.1724	£2 4 4

252

Date of indenture	Name of apprentice	Christian name of Father	Occupation of Father	Place of origin	Shipwright to whom apprenticed	Date of freedom	Price for freedom
3.10.1716	Benjamin Lotherington	Benjamin	Master Marriner	Whitby, Yorks.	William Trewhitt		
3.10.1716	Lyonel Robson	John	Yeoman	Newcastle	Peter Waite	7.4.1724	£2 4 4
13.4.1716	Thomas Cooper	John	Yeoman	Sunderland	Paul Hollyday		
11.2.1717	William Watson	James	Gent	Westlakeburn, Durham			
5.2.1717	Jacob Hedley	Robert	Yeoman	Upper Leam	Thomas Campion	27.12.1725	£2 15 5
12.2.1717	Joseph Turpin	Tho.	Gent	Northseaton	Tho. Reed sen.		
1.1.1717	Isaac Corney	Isaac	Glassmaker (decd)		Wm Trewhit	4.12.1724	£2 4 4
25.3.1717	Richard Watson	Anthony	Yeoman	London	Wm Wrangham		
2.5.1717	John Collinson	Henry	Gent	Tunstall, Durham	Thomas Wallas		
23.5.1717	John Angus	Robert	Gent	Newton	Thomas Campion		
27.12.1716	Robert Liddle [Lydell]			Cramlington	Paul Holliday		
11.6.1717	John Lettiney [Lattiney]	John	Marriner (decd)	Newcastle	Bryan Wall	7.4.1724	£2 4 4
4.4.1717	John Henderson	Jane	Yeoman	Newcastle	John Trewhitt	4.12.1724	£2 4 4
1.1.1718	Thomas Watson	Wm	Yeoman	Heworth, Durham	Edward Wilkinson	28.12.1724	£2 9 10
6.5.1718	Robert Young	Robert	Keelman	Howton-le-Spring, Durham	Thomas Wallas	29.9.1726	£2 5 4
24.4.1718	Mathew Sheatham	Robert	Yeoman	Newcastle	Tho. Wrangham	12.4.1726	£2 4 4
26.5.1718	John Haward	Wm	Gent (decd)	Low Heworth, Durham	Jeremiah Cooke / Paul Holliday		
23.3.1719	Ralph Lawson	John	Marriner	London	James Forster	18.1.1727	£2 14 4
28.4.1719	John Fawden	John	Gent (decd)	Branden, Durham	Joseph Campion	29.9.1726	£2 4 10

Date of indenture	Name of apprentice	Christian name of Father	Occupation of Father	Place of origin	Shipwright to whom apprenticed	Date of freedom	Price for freedom
7.1.1719	John Lee	William	Yeoman	Bedlington, Durham	Roger Durham jun.	29.9.1726	£4 4 4
25.5.1719	Wm Walker	John	Gent	Tinemouth	Wm Hanby		
22.9.1719	Thomas Marley	Ralph	Gent	North End, Lamsley, Durham	Thomas Campion		
10.4.1719	John Scott	Andrew	Yeoman	Newcastle	Wm Wrangham	27.12.1726	£2 15 4
5.1.1720	John Liddle [Liddell]	Alexander	Yeoman		Bryan Wall		
19.7.1720	Robert Young	Wm	Gent	South Sheilds, Durham	John Goodson	4.9.1727	£2 14 4
1.10.1719	Edward Fuller	Edward	Brickmaker	Chesle Hampton, Berkshire	Wm Wrangham		
16.1.1721	Mathew Watson	Mark	Boat Builder	North Sheilds	Edward Forster		
27.12.1720	Robert Milburn	Nicholas	Yeoman	Newcastle	Paul Halliday		
9.7.1717	William Thompson				Jeremiah Cook	27.12.1725	£2 14 4
20.4.1722	Ralph Ord		Yeoman	Longridge, Durham	Roger Durham	24.6.1728	£2 14 4
2.7.1722	Robert Metcalfe	John	Yeoman	Marske, Yorks.	Joseph Campion	29.4.1735	£2 12 6
26.11.1722	John Bebee	Robert	Yeoman	Newcastle	Cuthbert Preston	11.4.1732	£2 6 10
7.1.1723	James Dryden	George	(decd)	Newcastle	Thomas Wilson		
1.1.1723	Joseph Hay	Alexander	Yeoman	Newcastle	John Thoburn	24.6.1730	£2 14 10
16.12.1723	Robert Carr	Wm	Yeoman	Newcastle	John Waite	24.6.1730	£2 14 4
27.12.1725	David Carr	William	Gent	Chattoe, Scotland	Paul Holliday	19.2.1734	£2 14 2
25.6.1725	William Marshall	Robert	Marriner	Newcastle	William Trewhett		
12.4.1726	Thomas Johnson		Yeoman	Stanton	Cuthbert Preston	27.12.1733	£2 14 4
1.6.1726	Robert Stonehouse	Lawrence	Yeoman	Whitby, Yorks.	Joseph Campion	16.1.1734	£2 14 8

Date of indenture	Name of apprentice	Christian name of Father	Occupation of Father	Place of origin	Shipwright to whom apprenticed	Date of freedom	Price for freedom
2.8.1726	James Ians [Eyons]	John	Yeoman	East Sleekburn, Durham	John Lettiney	20.2.1734	£2 14 8
7.4.1726	Andrew Richardson	Robert	Yeoman	Doddiston, Scotland	William Hanby	*	
28.8.1727	Thomas Pattison	John	Yeoman	Benwell	Abraham Dowsey		
29.3.1727	John Brewhouse	Richard	Yeoman	Newcastle	Roger Durham	29.9.1735	£2 15 2
7.7.1727	Thomas Rutlish	Thos.	Yeoman	Allendale Town	Thomas Wallis	27.12.1734	£2 14 2
2.1.1727	Philip Moor	John	Plumber	Newcastle	William Trewhitt	27.12.1734	£2 14 2
6.4.1727	Peregrine Hutton	Wm	Gent	Pears Bridge, Durham	Edward Trewhitt		
14.2.1727	William Sanderson	Henry	Yeoman	Newcastle	William Hansby	12.2.1735	£2 14 2
29.9.1727	Robert Marlay	Ralph		Northends, Lamsley, Durham	Thomas Marlay		
10.3.1729	John Lasley [Lashley]	John	Yeoman	Newcastle	Bryan Wall		
16.2.1729	John Curry	Charles	Yeoman	Newcastle	Paul Halliday	24.6.1735	£2 12 2
13.5.1729	Thomas Berry	John	Marriner	North Sheilds	Robert Wallis		
20.5.1729	Thomas Hindson	John	Tobacconist	Bowes, Yorks.	Robert Wallis		
21.6.1729	Thomas Pearson	Michael	Pitman	Swards, Durham	Joseph Campion	30.8.1736	£2 12 0
6.10.1729	John Harrison	Henry	Master Marriner	Newcastle	John Thorbourne	12.4.1737	£2 14 2
11.11.1729	Thos. Dixon	Thos.		Hartley	Thos. Dixon	21.12.1737	£2 14 2
14.1.1730	Thomas Wilkinson	George	Yeoman	Gateshead	Thos. Harrison	4.8.1738	£2 15 10
14.1.1730	Michael Mackintosh	John	Yeoman	Newcastle	Thos. Harrison	10.8.1738	£2 12 0
2.2.1730	John Reed	Alexander	Yeoman	Newcastle	Cuthbert Preston	27.10.1740	£2 12 2
14.4.1730	Ralph Crow	Christopher	Yeoman	Jarrow, Durham	Roger Durham	27.12.1737	£2 14 2
1.4.1730	Robert Gothard	Stephen	Keelman	Newcastle	William Henderson	21.8.1738	£2 14 2

Date of indenture	Name of apprentice	Christian name of Father	Occupation of Father	Place of origin	Shipwright to whom apprenticed	Date of freedom	Price for freedom
2.6.1731	James Wilkinson	William	Yeoman	Reedrow, Durham	Thomas Wallis		
17.11.1731	Thomas Galley	Ralph	Tailor	Beemish, Durham	Thos. Wallis jun.	1.12.1739	£2 12 2
1.12.1731	John Smith			Newcastle	William Trewhit	21.10.1739	£2 12 2
2.7.1732	Robert Lyons	James	Yeoman	Newcastle	Robert Wallis		
11.9.1732	James Young	James	Yeoman	Newcastle	George Wilson		
20.7.1730	Willm Kirton	Mattw	Gent	Haneley	John Lettiney		
22.3.1733	Robert Jackson	George	Tailor	Newcastle	John Lee		
28.3.1733	Henry Johnson	Robert	Miller	Stanton	Ralph Ord		
8.1.1734	John Goddard	Stephen	Keelman	Newcastle	Joseph Campion	24.6.1741	£2 12 2
8.1.1734	Edward Laing	Robert	Yeoman	Annesford	Edward Trewhitt	24.6.1741	£2 12 2
5.1.1734	Thomas Suddes	John	Yeoman	Red Raw, Durham			
16.4.1734	Richard Shaw	Richard	Customs Officer	Holy Island, Durham	Thomas Marley	27.12.1744	£2 13 2
26.4.1734	Richard Bonner				Robert Storey		
3.2.1736	Joseph Naylor	Andrew	Yeoman	Newcastle	Robert Wallis		
4.3.1736	Robert Wheatley	John	Shipwright	Newcastle	Robt Coulson		
29.12.1737	William Smith	John	Yeoman	Links Green, Durham	Thomas Marley		
13.4.1737	John Wilson	John	Joyner	Howick	Cuthbert [?]	25.6.1744	£2 12 2
29.3.1738	William Gaire	Richard	Yeoman	Cackfordlaw	John Thowburn	4.3.1746	£2 14 2
29.6.1738	Roger Almory	Henry	Weaver	Gateshead	Robert Coulson	27.12.1745	£2 13 2
7.11.1738	Joseph Thompson	Richard	Marriner	Gateshead	John Turnbull		
13.8.1737	William Ramsey	David	House-carpenter	Alnmouth	Ralph Lowson		
20.1.1739	John Tomlin	John	Gent (decd)	Greys, Essex	Thomas Marley		
3.12.1739	Stephen Gothart	Stephen	Yeoman	Newcastle	George Muris / Robert Gothart		

Date of indenture	Name of apprentice	Christian name of Father	Occupation of Father	Place of origin	Shipwright to whom apprenticed	Date of freedom	Price for freedom
23.8.1740	Jacob Fisher	Thos.	Wheelwright (decd)	Newcastle	William Henderson		
16.8.1740	Gabriel Coal	Gabriel	Yeoman	Blackburn Moor, Durham			
3.8.1739	John Renoldson	William	Shipwright	Newcastle	Thos. Marley		
23.1.1741	William Laing	Thomas	Mariner	Newcastle	Thos. Marley		
2.2.1741	William Clarke	Cliffe		North Shields	John Thouburn	17.1.1749	£2 12 8
2.12.1740	John Banner	Richard	Customs Officer	Craster	Robert Liddell		
3.9.1741	Thomas Teasdale	John	Shoemaker	Aldston Moor, Cumberland	Robert Storey		
9.5.1741	John Gibson	Ralph	Miller	Newcastle	John Bruce [Brewhouse]	29.4.1749	£2 12 8
5.1.1743	Ephraim Currey	William	Yeoman	Dentshole	Robert Coulson	21.2.1749	£2 12 2
8.4.1743	John Almory	Henry	Weaver	Gateshead	Edward Trewhitt	29.9.1751	£2 13 2
23.5.1743	John Clough	Phillip	Yeoman	Hopscod	John Thowburn	29.9.1750	£2 13 8
17.10.1743	Thomas Goddart	Stephen	Yeoman	Newcastle	Robert Wallis		
22.8.1743	Bartholomew Barker	George	Ropemaker	Newcastle	John Goddart	9.4.1751	£2 12 2
19.4.1744	George Smith	Henry	Master & Mariner	South Shields, Durham	John Burrell	9.4.1751	£2 13 9
4.5.1744	John Salkeld	George	Farmer	Lesbury	Philip Moore	27.12.1751	£2 16 8
6.6.1744	Bailey Brown	Alexander	Innkeeper	Newcastle	Robert Storey	*	
2.10.1744	William Carss	James	Mariner	Newcastle	James Eyons	16.2.1753	£2 18 8
9.7.1745	Joseph Claxton	Edward	Yeoman (decd)	Newcastle	Andrew Haxton	31.3.1752	£2 14 8
1.11.1745	John Ellison	Robert	Yeoman	Wallsend	John Fawdon	8.2.1753	£2 15 6
19.10.1745	Ridley Cuthbertson	Ridley	Barber	Warkworth	Francis Trewhitt / Ralph Lawson	26.10.1753	£2 14 8

Date of indenture	Name of apprentice	Christian name of Father	Occupation of Father	Place of origin	Shipwright to whom apprenticed	Date of freedom	Price for freedom
21.1.1746	Joseph Turpin	Joseph	Shipwright (decd)	Newcastle	William Henderson	31.3.1752	£3 5 2
27.1.1746	George Hedley	John	Yeoman	Newcastle	William Henderson	5.6.1754	£2 15 8
12.2.1746	Robert Smith	John	Yeoman	Ravensworth, Durham	John Carrier	*	
14.5.1746	Thomas Henzell	John	Glassmaker	Newcastle	Edward Trewhitt	8.10.1753	£2 12 2
29.5.1746	William Pearson	James	Yeoman	Newcastle	William Watson	14.2.1754	£2 13 8
20.6.1746	George Johnson	John	Yeoman	Newcastle	Robert Gothard		
7.1.1747	Joseph Barker	Joseph	Gardner	Craister	Robert Liddell		
4.5.1747	John Hall	Anthony	Yeoman (decd)	Newcastle	Cuthbert Preston		
1.9.1747	George Cram	George	Yeoman	Dentshole	William Wilkinson jun.	22.12.1755	£2 15 2
11.11.1747	John Paterson	Stephen	Yeoman	Howick	Phillip Moore		
10.10.1747	William Ramsey	William	Gent	Berham Leazes, Durham	Enoch White	27.12.1756	£2 18 8
26.5.1747	Benjamin Banner	Richard		Dunston Steeds, Embleton	Robert Storey	27.12.1755	£2 17 8
10.6.1748	Thomas Curry	Ralph	Yeoman	Ouseburn	Bryan Wall	27.12.1755	£2 12 2
4.10.1748	Thomas Allen	Robert	Mariner	Newcastle	Edward Trewhit	27.12.1756	£3 15 2
5.10.1748	Thomas Brown	Michaell	Yeoman	North Shields	Philip Moor		
24.6.1748	Robert Coulson		(decd)	Liverpool, Lancs.	Robert Liddell	21.12.1756	£2 14 8
16.1.1749	Christopher Henzell	Moses	Glassmaker (decd)	Newcastle	William Charlton		
21.2.1749	John Ridley	William	Mariner (decd)	Newcastle	Edward Laing	27.1.1757	£2 17 2
11.4.1749	Thomas Levison	John	Waterman	Newcastle	John Goddart	†	
5.5.1749	John Rogers	Joseph	Yeoman	Newcastle	John Renoldson	*	

258

Date of indenture	Name of apprentice	Christian name of Father	Occupation of Father	Place of origin	Shipwright to whom apprenticed	Date of freedom	Price for freedom
1.11.1749	Thomas Ravens	Thomas	Mariner (decd)	Northshields	Roger Almory		
25.10.1749	Robert Smith	Robert	Yeoman	Newcastle	William Marshall		
23.1.1750	William Cuthbert	George	Blacksmith (decd)				
2.4.1750	Joseph Emmerson	John	Yeoman	Lamesly, Durham	John Carrier		
10.4.1750	Jacob Lee	Jacob	Marriner	Dentshole North Blyth, Durham	Edward Trewhitt	*	
3.2.1750	William Crawford	William	Sinker (decd)	Newcastle	William Charlton		
7.5.1750	Thomas Robinson	Thomas	Yeoman	Embleton	Stephen Goddard		
30.5.1750	Joseph Moor	Walter	Waterman	Newcastle	Thomas Taylor		
13.6.1750	William Adon	Luke	Marriner (decd)	Newcastle	William Watson	27.12.1757	£2 15 8
1.3.1750	William Dawson			North Shields	John Fawdon		
29.10.1750	George Hedley	Wm	Yeoman	Newcastle	William Staward		
31.1.1751	John Brydon	John	Overman	Denton	Francis Trewhitt	31.3.1762	£3 8 2
10.2.1751	Benjamin Brass	Wm	Yeoman	Newcastle	John Turnbull	29.9.1760	£3 1 2
1.2.1751	James Harbottle	Thomas	Skinner & Glover	Newcastle	Ralph Lowson		
18.2.1751	Ratcliffe Ottaway	Robert	Yeoman	Newcastle	Ralph Crow	*	
10.1.1751	Parsewell Hedley	Geo.	Yeoman	Newcastle	Paul Park		
15.4.1751	John Johnson	Michael	Yeoman (decd)	North Middleton	John Reynoldson	*	
11.4.1751	William Donkin	John	Waterman	Newcastle	James Eyons	29.12.1758	£2 14 8
25.3.1751	Robert Bowart	John (decd)		Newcastle	John Goddard	27.9.1759	£4 16 2
25.10.1751	Edward Walton	John		Byker	Roger Almory	†	
3.10.1751	John Dixon	Joseph	Sailor (decd)	London	Stephen Gothart Luke Younghusband	*	

259

Date of indenture	Name of apprentice	Christian name of Father	Occupation of Father	Place of origin	Shipwright to whom apprenticed	Date of freedom	Price for freedom
16.1.1752	Wm Ridley	Wm	Marriner (decd)	Newcastle	Edwd Trewhitt		
1.1.1752	John Spencer	Thos.	House-carpenter (decd)				
11.6.1752	Francis Wardale	Thos.	Keelman	Newcastle	John Carrier	25.6.1759	£2 12 2
19.5.1752	James Crosby	James	Yeoman	Fryars Goose, Durham	Bryan Wall	29.9.1760	£2 12 8
4.5.1752	Robt Wilson	Thos.	Master & Marriner		Wm Wilkinson		
18.5.1752	Charles Watson	Wm	Smith (decd)	Newcastle	Robt Gothard	27.12.1759	£2 12 2
4.5.1752	Cuthbert Graham	Cuth.	Weaver	Newcastle	Francis Trewhitt	14.1.1760	£2 15 2
21.4.1752	Isaac Scott	John	Glassman	Newcastle	John Reynoldson	30.6.1760	£2 15 8
13.4.1752	John Urwin	Wm	Maltster	Newcastle	Robt French	*	
1.5.1752	Henry Doeg	Henry	Keelman	Newcastle	Wm Laing	*	
29.6.1752	Robert Huntley	Thos.	Gent	Burdon, Durham	Wm Reynoldson	27.12.1759	£2 13 2
3.11.1752	John Temple	James	Yeoman	Newcastle	Wm Charlton		
2.10.1752	Wm Reavely	James	Gent (decd)	Almouth	Enoch White		
18.1.1753	Lancelot Fairbarns	Robt	Corver	Ouseburn	Wm Wilkinson	*	
11.8.1753	John Lawson	George	Yeoman	Backworth	James White		
3.9.1753	John Cleugh	John	Gent (decd)	Winlington, Durham	Edwd Trewhit		
28.12.1753	Joseph Nixon	Joseph	Dyer	Gateshead	John Gothart	28.12.1772	£6 19 2
30.9.1754	Thos. Clark				John Headlam	*	
30.9.1754	Geo. Pattison				John Headlam		
30.9.1754	John Routlidge				John Headlam		
30.9.1754	George Hadon				John Headlam		
30.9.1754	William Ostens				John Headlam	26.4.1756	£4 12 2

Date of indenture	Name of apprentice	Christian name of Father	Occupation of Father	Place of origin	Shipwright to whom apprenticed	Date of freedom	Price for freedom
30.9.1754	Joseph Wright				John Headlam		
30.9.1754	Christopher Watson	Francis	Yeoman	Newcastle	John Headlam	27.12.1762	£2 15 2
1.5.1755	Thomas Hobkirk	James	Yeoman	Greatham, Durham	Roger Almory		
25.3.1756	John Hett				John Headlam		
2.4.1756	David Wallace	David	Master & Marriner	Arbroath, Scotland	John Headlam	*	
6.4.1756	Robert Henderson	John	Keelman	Newcastle	John Headlam		
19.1.1756	Richard Sanderson	Wm	Corver	Newcastle	Roger Almory		
31.12.1755	Simon Hutchinson	Simon	Master & Marriner	South Shields, Durham	George Smith		
3.1.1757	Robt Fowler	Walter	Yeoman (decd)	Middleham in Tividale, Scotland	George Smith		
12.4.1757	Wm Blackey	Robt	Waterman	Newcastle	E. Trewhitt		
18.1.1757	Ralph Barkas	Thos.	Yeoman	Heddon on the Wall	Wm Wilkinson		
27.3.1758	George Thornton	George	Tailor	Stannington	Enoch White		
28.2.1758	George Scotland	George	Yeoman	Newcastle	Wm Wilkinson		
14.2.1758	Andrew Cram	George	Waterman	Dentshole	John Coxen		
1.8.1757	William Stokoe	Sarah	(Widow)	Hexham	George Cram		
20.2.1758	John White	Alexander	Glassman	Newcastle	George Smith		
2.5.1757	Matthew Pearson	Caleb	Yeoman	Fallowden	John Gothard		
4.9.1758	Jonathan Cram	Geo.	Yeoman	Dentshole	John Headlam		
7.7.1757	Willm Hewitt	Peter	Fisherman	Northshields	Geo. Lidle		

Date of indenture	Name of apprentice	Christian name of Father	Occupation of Father	Place of origin	Shipwright to whom apprenticed	Date of freedom	Price for freedom
26.1.1758	Thos. Hall	Thos.	Yeoman	Newcastle	Roger Almory		
13.6.1758	Ralph Storey	George	Surgeon	Chester in the Street, Durham	Roger Almory		
30.9.1758	Thomas Gibson	Ralph	Yeoman (decd)	Chester in the Street, Durham	Roger Almory		
1.1.1759	William Cook	John	Butcher	Newcastle	John Gibson		
15.11.1758	Robert Brown	William	House-carpenter		John Carryer	27.12.1765	£2 12 2
22.1.1759	Mathew Henderson	Mark	Yeoman	Wylam	John Headlam	14.4.1786	£6 12 2
12.2.1759	Robert Rankain	Robert	Yeoman	Newcastle	Roger Almory	6.1.1769	£3 2 8
26.3.1759	Richard Scott	John	Marriner	Newcastle	Roger Almory		
6.4.1759	William Stewart	Charles	Wheelwright	South Shields, Durham	Edward Trewhitt	1.4.1766	£2 12 2
1.6.1759	John Graham	Richard	Joiner	Jarrow, Durham	George Renoldson		
1.1.1759	Ralph Gibson	Ralph	Yeoman	South Shields	Francis Trewhitt		
2.7.1759	Charles Duffe	Dougall	Yeoman (decd)	Chester in the Street, Durham	John Gibson		
1.3.1760	Andrew Gibson	Thomas	Innkeeper	Newcastle	Francis Trewhitt		
1.8.1759	John Marshall	John	Yeoman	Newcastle	Michael Mackintosh		
1.1.1760	John Pearsey	Willm	Innkeeper	South Shields	George Smith		
10.4.1760	John Heslop	George	Yeoman	Newcastle	James White		
				Newcastle	Edward Trewhitt		

Date of indenture	Name of apprentice	Christian name of Father	Occupation of Father	Place of origin	Shipwright to whom apprenticed	Date of freedom	Price for freedom
7.7.1760	Thomas Moorhead	Finley Clark (father in law)					
18.10.1759	William Otway	Robert	Yeoman	Sandgate	Edward Trewhitt		
9.6.1760	Isaac Spark	Robert	Yeoman	Newcastle	William Carss		
1.7.1760	Richard Brown	George	Master & Marriner (decd)	Byker	John Park		
12.7.1760	Henry Reed	Thomas	Yeoman	Gateshead	T. E. Headlam		
30.9.1760	Francis Hopkirk	Francis	Innkeeper	Newburn	John Almory		
11.5.1761	George Johnson	John	Marriner	Newcastle	John Almory		
15.6.1761	Solomon Smith	George	Marriner	Dentshole	John Spenser		
24.8.1761	Christopher Green	Christopher	Yeoman (decd)	Newcastle	Thomas Currey		
26.4.1762	Thomas Taylor	Joseph	Yeoman	Gateshead	Thomas Currey		
13.5.1762	John Leighton	Thomas	Yeoman	Gateshead	T. E. Headlam		
15.2.1763	William Robson	Henry	Waterman	Newcastle	John Sempell jun.		
22.2.1763	Matthew Watson	James	Marriner	Newcastle	Edward Laing		
9.5.1763	Thomas Edgar	Martin	Innkeeper	Newcastle	George Hedley		
8.11.1762	George Wilson	William	(decd)	Newcastle	William Rennoldson		
3.5.1762	Ralph Davison	William	Waggon-wright	South Shields, Durham	George Smith		
18.7.1763	Robert Cunningham	John	Waterman	Whickham, Durham	Thomas Curry		
26.10.1762	Thomas Guthery	Thomas	Yeoman	Newcastle	John Thackery		
18.10.1763	Richard Moorhead	Thomas	Waterman (decd)	Newcastle	William Thoburn	3.2.1783	£5 9 8
				Newcastle	Joseph Moore		

Date of indenture	Name of apprentice	Christian name of Father	Occupation of Father	Place of origin	Shipwright to whom apprenticed	Date of freedom	Price for freedom
28.7.1763	Andrew Wake	Thomas	Yeoman	Benwell	John Coxon		
1.3.1763	John Oxnard	Edward	Gent	Mickleton, Yorks.	John Gothard		
26.12.1763	William Thew	William	Yeoman	Stannington	William Wilkinson		
31.5.1762	Alexander Thoburn	James	Keelman	Newcastle	John Rennoldson		
2.6.1763	Joseph Brown	Bignell	Wright	Northumberland	John Rennoldson	5.10.1801	£5 0 0
12.8.1763	David Lourieston	David	Yeoman	Newcastle	John Gothard		
7.5.1764	William Bowie	George	Innkeeper	Newcastle	William Charlton		
1.11.1763	William Cowley	William	Waggon-wright				
7.2.1764	John Richardson	John	Yeoman	Redheugh, Durham	John Spencer		
24.9.1764	Matthew Fairlam	Michael	Staithman	Newcastle	John Coxon		
3.9.1764	Robert Coxon	Edward	Glassmaker	Heworth, Durham	William Charlton		
7.6.1764	John Kemp	John	Keelman	Newcastle	Edward Trewhit		
20.10.1764	John Bell	William	Innkeeper	Harlowhill	Robert Wilson	*	
11.12.1764	William Metcalfe	William	Joiner	North Shields	Edward Trewhitt	6.10.1776	£3 14 2
22.12.1764	James Johnson	Gawine	Bowlmaker	Weldon Hall	Edward Trewhitt		
27.9.1764	Cuthbert Orrick	George	Maltmaker	Newcastle	Edward Trewhitt		
3.7.1764	William Wilson	William		Heaton Watermill	George Smith	*	
14.11.1764	William Collingwood	Robert	Yeoman	Hedworth, Durham	John Coxon		
7.5.1764	Wm Lambert	Lancelot	Wheelwright	Framlington	George Smith	27.12.1776	£3 18 2
7.5.1764	Edward Howie	John	Yeoman	Eglingham	Robert Wilson	29.9.1775	£3 6 2
27.2.1765	Thomas Ward Douglass	Robert	Master & Marriner	South Shore, Gateshead	Robert Wilson / Edward Trewhitt	29.9.1772	£2 16 2

Date of indenture	Name of apprentice	Christian name of Father	Occupation of Father	Place of origin	Shipwright to whom apprenticed	Date of freedom	Price for freedom
9.10.1764	Henry Marshall	Henry	Gardener	Newcastle	John Semple jun.		
1.2.1764	James Wilson	James	Baker	Newcastle	William Carse		
19.11.1764	William Lundy			Newcastle	John Rennoldson		
4.8.1758	John Armstrong	Robert	Yeoman	North Shields	William Charleton		
9.3.1759	George Wright	Francis	Master & Marriner		William Charleton		
26.4.1765	Thomas Lander	Joseph	Gardner	South Blyth	George Maughling		
17.4.1764	Edward Potts	Edward	Labourer	Gateshead	John Rennoldson		
26.8.1765	John Park	James	Keelman	Newcastle	Thomas Taylor sen.		
8.5.1765	Alexander Moorehead	Thomas	(decd)	Newcastle	John Almory		
14.12.1765	Hilton Tinker	John	Master & Marriner	Newcastle	George Smith		
1.1.1765	George Blakey	Robert	Waterman	South Shields, Durham	William Wilkinson		
19.11.1764	Henry Carter	Henry	Yeoman (decd)	Newcastle	John Spencer		
1.3.1760	Caleb Pearson	Caleb	Yeoman	Newcastle	T. E. Headlam		
3.6.1760	Thomas Storey	Robert	Yeoman	Fallowdon	George Smith		
11.8.1764	Jacob Keedy	John	Keelman	South Shields	Robert Wilson	*	
14.1.1765	John Olliver	Thomas	Keelman	Newcastle	Robert Wilson	*	
16.8.1765	Thomas Garret	Thomas	Farmer (decd)	Newcastle	T. E. Headlam		
13.2.1764	John Rayne	William	Yeoman	Woodhorn	John Gothard		
3.1.1765	William Gillery	William	Weaver	Mickleton, Yorks.	John Gothard		
29.9.1766	Thomas Scott	John	Marriner	Newcastle	Richard Scott	27.12.1773	£2 16 2
29.1.1767	Matthew Pringle	Edward	Baker	South Shields	William Carse	14.1.1774	£2 12 2
29.5.1765	Alexander Fenwick (late a charity boy of All Saints, Newcastle)				Joseph Edgar		
1.7.1763	Alexander Irwin	John	Keelman	Newcastle	Francis Trewhitt		

265

Date of indenture	Name of apprentice	Christian name of Father	Occupation of Father	Place of origin	Shipwright to whom apprenticed	Date of freedom	Price for freedom
22.8.1769	James Wilson	John	Yeoman	Newcastle	William Charleton	26.4.1780	£3 6 2¼
4.1.1771	James Evans	James	Shipwright	South Shields	Richard Scott	11.7.1780	£3 2 2¼
9.7.1771	John Laing	William	Yeoman	Scotland	William Carse		
26.10.1771	William Stephenson	John	Weaver	Lamesly, Durham	Thomas Curry		
27.2.1772	William Carncross	John	Yeoman	Newcastle	Thomas Curry		
27.4.1772	Thomas Pearson	Bryan	Yeoman	Gateshead	T. E. Headlam	*	
1.7.1771	William Walker	John	Baker	South Shields, Durham			
11.5.1772	Nicholas Havelock	Nicholas	Corfmaker	Birtley, Durham	George Smith		
27.6.1772	George Blackburd	George		Chester by Calling, Durham	Thomas Curry		
1.9.1772	Robert Mills	Isaac	Breeches-maker		John Rennoldson		
9.3.1773	Thomas Cox	Thomas	Leather dresser	Newcastle	Thomas Curry	*	
10.3.1773	George Wray	John	Gent	Newcastle Teams, Gateshead	Thomas Curry		
30.12.1773	Thomas Hearn	John	Shipwright	North Shields	George Smith	2.4.1782	£2 18 2
7.7.1750	James Storey	John	Yeoman	North Shields	William Carse	15.1.1781	£2 12 2
1.11.1774	Charles Stuart	Ralph	Yeoman	Gateshead	John Bruce	2.10.1775	£2 16 2
4.11.1776	William Gamsby	George	Farmer (decd)	Gateshead	T. E. Headlam	27.12.1782	£2 14 2
29.9.1777	John Turner	Andrew	Keelman (decd)		John Almory	27.12.1784	
18.12.1776	Joseph Watson	William	Corn Merchant	Newcastle	John Rennoldson	27.12.1785	£2 16 2
1.9.1777	William Embleton	Robert	Farmer	Easington	T. E. Headlam		
22.4.1778	Simon Temple	Simon	Shipwright	Bambrough, South Shields	T. E. Headlam, George Smith	10.4.1787	£3 0 2

Date of indenture	Name of apprentice	Christian name of Father	Occupation of Father	Place of origin	Shipwright to whom apprenticed	Date of freedom	Price for freedom
21.4.1778	Thomas Wiggam	Thomas	Farmer	Byker	William Laslie		
28.4.1777	William Headlam	Charles		Gateshead	T. E. Headlam		
[?]	William Charlton				Wm Trewhitt	27.12.1777	£4 12 2
10.3.1777	Robert Benson	William	Mariner	North Shore, Newcastle	Thomas Curry		
1.10.1777	George Young	Luke	Yeoman	Lowlights, Tynemouth	Thomas Curry	28.12.1801	£5 0 0
24.6.1778	Thomas Forsyth	Thos.	Shipwright	South Shields	Wm Charlton jun.	27.12.1785	£2 12 2
14.8.1778	Joseph Henry Harding	Joseph	Shipwright	Tynemouth	James Storey		
15.9.1777	William Wright	Roger	Mariner	Gateshead	T. E. Headlam		
9.9.1778	Henry Charlton	Henry	Farmer	Aydon	John Bell	24.6.1799	£5 0 0
26.6.1778	Archibald Irwin	Archibald	Cordwainer	Sandgate	William Carss		
10.8.1778	William Bowness	John	Blacksmith	Allenheads	Thomas Curry		
30.9.1778	Henry Wright	William	Marriner (decd)				
27.3.1778	Thomas Simm	Andrew	Brewer	Shore Side, Newcastle	John Almory	27.12.1785	£2 12 2
[?]	William Laslie			Newcastle	Thomas Curry		
11.7.1780	James Atkinson	Robert	Farmer	Brickwood Hall	John Trewhitt	22.4.1778	£3 15 8½
28.8.1780	James Robertson	James	Yeoman	Newcastle	James Evans jun.		
3.8.1779	Ralph Procter	William	Yeoman	Newcastle	William Carss	1.10.1804	£5 0 0
29.4.1780	Ralph Turnbull	James	Shipwright	Shore Side, Newcastle	Thomas Curry		
30.5.1780	Robert Lambert	Thomas	Wheelwright	Rothbury	William Laslie		
16.5.1780	John Oliver	James	Keelman (decd)		William Laslie		
19.3.1781	Joseph Carter	Cornelius	Waterman	Sandgate Newcastle	John Remoldson Thomas Curry	†	

267

Date of indenture	Name of apprentice	Christian name of Father	Occupation of Father	Place of origin	Shipwright to whom apprenticed	Date of freedom	Price for freedom
26.12.1780	John Wood	Joseph	Shipwright	Lowlights, Tynemouth	James Storey		
1.5.1781	Thomas Buck	Francis	Shipwright	North Shields	James Storey		
11.11.1779	William Headlam	Anthony	Farmer	Iggleston, Durham	T. E. Headlam		
21.8.1781	Thomas Pattison	Thomas	Waterman	Shore Side, Newcastle	Thomas Curry	22.10.1788	£6 12 2
25.11.1780	James Mackenzie	Kennet	Yeoman (decd)	Newcastle	William Laslie		
11.6.1781	William Lawson	Robert	Marriner	Ballast Hills, Newcastle	James Evans		
18.3.1782	William Kay	Bartholomew	Shipwright	North Shields	Thomas Hearn		
26.10.1781	Henry Swan	Henry	Farmer (decd)	Wallsend	William Laslie	2.5.1791	£3 0 2
2.8.1782	James Russell	John	Yeoman	Newcastle	William Laslie		
1.11.1782	Andrew Turner	Andrew	Keelman	Newcastle	John Reynoldson		
26.2.1783	William Wood	David	Keelman	Newcastle	William Carss		
10.3.1783	Robert Guthrie	Thomas	Shipwright	Newcastle	His father		
14.10.1783	Joseph Coxon	Henry	Overman	Ballast Hills	John Rennoldson	27.12.1804	£5 0 0
20.2.1784	Joseph Hearn	John	Shipbuilder	North Shields	Thomas Hearn	2.5.1791	£2 12 2
4.4.1782	Nicholas Blackett	George	Shipwright	Gateshead	T. E. Headlam		
16.9.1784	John Laverick	Eli	Shipwright	Lowlights, Tynemouth	Thomas Hearn		
23.4.1783	James Carse	George	Mariner	Newcastle	Thomas Curry	27.12.1804	£5 0 0
19.4.1784	Matthew Soulsby	Michael	Viewer	Hedley Fell	T. E. Headlam		
7.2.1785	Edward Drury	John	House-carpenter	London	James Evans		
8.3.1783	Robert Smith	Robert	Sawyer	Ewesburn	Thomas Curry		
28.4.1785	Fargus Walker	Ninian	Mariner	Shore Side	William Carss		

Date of indenture	Name of apprentice	Christian name of Father	Occupation of Father	Place of origin	Shipwright to whom apprenticed	Date of freedom	Price for freedom
23.7.1785	Jacob Venus	Jacob	Mariner	North Shields	Thomas Hearn		
27.6.1785	George Bell	William	Victualler	Newcastle	William Carss		
1.8.1785	Thomas Brown	Joseph	Husbandman	Cunninggarth	William Carss	*	
14.3.1785	William Oxnet	John	Keelman	Ouzeburn	William Laslie		
26.6.1786	William Wright	William	Master Marriner (decd)	North Shore, Newcastle			
26.6.1786	John Hemsley	William	Farmer	West Acomb	Henry Wright	24.6.1807	£5 0 0
7.6.1786	Thomas Harle	John	Farmer	Newcastle	John Bell		
28.4.1787	William Smith	Matthew	Mariner	South Shields, Durham	William Laslie	27.12.1796	£5 0 0
12.5.1785	Alexander Petrie	Alexander	Gardiner (decd)	Sandgate	John Bell		
25.7.1785	William Hunter	Joseph	Gent	Byker Hill	Thomas Curry		
6.1.1786	John Temple	George	Shipwright	Newcastle	Thomas Curry		
12.1.1786	John Fife	John	Victualler	Newcastle	Thomas Curry		
25.6.1787	John Ingham	John	Gluemaker	Gateshead	Thomas Curry		
4.6.1787	Thomas Williamson	John	Mariner	North Shields	T. E. Headlam		
25.3.1788	Caleb Robson	William	Shipwright	Newcastle	George Cram		
1.5.1788	Richard Shaw Storey	James	Shipwright	Newcastle	Alexander Doag		
8.5.1787	John Macleod	John	Beer Brewer	Gateshead	His father		
1.4.1788	Peter Hoggins	Robert	Yeoman	Newcastle	William Laslie	13.10.1794	£2 12 2
25.6.1788	William Bell	William	Innkeeper	Newcastle	Robert Gothard		
23.10.1788	George Lee	John	Alehouse Keeper	Newcastle	John Bell		
4.6.1789	George Detchon	Roger	Tailor	Sandgate	Thomas Pattison		
4.6.1789	Thomas Sharp	James	Yeoman	North Shields	Thomas Hearne		

Date of indenture	Name of apprentice	Christian name of Father	Occupation of Father	Place of origin	Shipwright to whom apprenticed	Date of freedom	Price for freedom
8.6.1789	William Moberley	Richard	Upholsterer	Stepney, Middlesex	William Laslie		
22.5.1790	John Dodd	Hannah (widow)		Newcastle	Simon Temple		
19.5.1790	George Duncan	Thomas	Mariner	Sandgate Newcastle	Thomas Pattison	30.9.1799	£3 6 2
9.8.1790	William Stott	Joseph	Yeoman	Newcastle	William Laslie		
8.3.1791	Bernard Shaw	Bernard		Lowlesworth, Durham	William Lambert		
1.4.1791	Thompson Pearson	Francis	Grocer	South Shields, Durham	Thomas Forsyth		
1.4.1791	James Forsyth	Thomas	Shipwright (decd)	South Shields, Durham	Thomas Forsyth		
1.11.1791	Andrew Fleck	Andrew	Pitman	Walker	George Cram		
26.5.1790	Henry Barkas	George	Yeoman (decd)	Dunston Bank, Durham	T. E. Headlam		
28.3.1791	William Seymour	Henry	Yeoman	High Team, Durham	T. E. Headlam		
26.3.1792	Thomas Tase	William	Mariner	North Shields	Thomas Hearn		
3.4.1792	John Reed	James	Yeoman (decd)	North Shore, Newcastle	George Cram	27.12.1804	£4 18 2
1.7.1792	Edward Newton Armstrong	John	Yeoman	Castle Garth	Thomas Pattison	*	

Date of indenture	Name of apprentice	Christian name of Father	Occupation of Father	Place of origin	Shipwright to whom apprenticed	Date of freedom	Price for freedom
30.11.1793	James Kyd	Alexander	Major in corps of Engineers, East India Company	Bengal			
2.5.1792	Francis Jefferson	Francis	Master Mariner	South Shields	Thomas Hearne	*	
21.10.1793	William Francis Sammons	Robert	Ropemaker	Southwark, Surrey	Simon Temple jun.	*	
1.8.1793	John Horsley	John	Mariner (decd)	North Shields	Simon Temple jun.		
31.7.1793	William Nixon	William	Brewer	Newcastle	Thomas Hearne	*	
16.6.1791	Thomas Dodd	Hannah (widow)			William Laslie		
14.3.1794	George Hodgson	John	Miner (decd)	Newcastle	Simon Temple jun.	*	
8.10.1793	Thomas Simpson	Thomas	Publican (decd)	Aldstone	Thomas Pattison		
25.1.1794	Robert Thompson	Robert	Mariner	Sandgate	Robert Gothard		
25.1.1794	John Thompson	Anthony	Mariner	Newcastle	Robert Gothard		
25.1.1794	Alexander Proctor	John	Yeoman	Newcastle	Robert Gothard		
25.1.1794	William Bell	Thomas	Cordwainer	Newcastle	Robert Gothard		
17.5.1794	John Selkirk	John	Overman	Wallsend	Robert Gothard		
2.4.1794	William Liddell	George	Waterman	Mushroom Glasshouses, Newcastle	Thomas Hearn	*	
					William Laslie		

Date of indenture	*Name of apprentice*	*Christian name of Father*	*Occupation of Father*	*Place of origin*	*Shipwright to whom apprenticed*	*Date of freedom*	*Price for freedom*
22.11.1794	Robert Kyd	Alexander	Major	Bengal	Thomas Hearn	*	
13.7.1795	Matthias Dunn	Richard	Master Mariner	New Road, Newcastle			
19.9.1796	Thomas Duncan	Thomas	Mariner	Sandgate	Robert Gothard		
12.8.1797	Thomas Sadlers	Robert	Wherryman	Swalwell, Durham	Henry Wright	1.10.1804	£2 12 2
13.8.1798	John Gilchrist	John	Mariner	Saint Anthony's	Henry Wright	27.12.1813	£2 12 2
24.6.1799	Henry Charlton	John	Shipwright	Gateshead	Wm Laslie		
18.4.1799	Robinson Sutton	Robinson	Yeoman	Ouseburn	John Bell		
31.3.1800	Thomas Gibson	William	Shipwright	Newcastle	William Laslie	27.12.1806	£2 12 2
31.3.1800	William Henzell	Wm	Glassmaker	Newcastle	William Laslie		
21.1.1800	William Wheatley	John	Yeoman	Newcastle	William Laslie		
11.6.1800	Robert Sadler	John	Yeoman	Ballast Hills, Newcastle	Lionel Robson		
15.8.1800	John Temperley	Nicholas	Farmer	Brokenhaugh	George Cram		
7.10.1800	George Elliott	William	Bottlemaker	North Shore	Robert Gothard		
4.10.1800	Henry Doeg	Stephen	Master Mariner	North Shore	William Laslie		
4.10.1800	Stephen Doeg	Stephen	Master Mariner	North Shore	Alexander Doeg		
7.10.1801	Ratcliff Thomas Manchester	Ratcliff	Master Mariner	Newcastle	Alexander Doeg		
9.11.1801	Robson Davidson	Luke		North Shore	William Laslie		
25.6.1801	Wm Curry	Ralph		North Shore	Wm Carss		
1.2.1802	Thomas Adams	John		Ballast Hills	Wm Carss		
30.4.1802	Peter Armour	Peter	Master Mariner	Sandgate	Robert Gothard		

Date of indenture	Name of apprentice	Christian name of Father	Occupation of Father	Place of origin	Shipwright to whom apprenticed	Date of freedom	Price for freedom
24.6.1802	John Clark	Edward	Cartman	Sandgate	Robert Gothard		
20.7.1802	John Christopher Morris	William	Mariner	North Shore Newcastle	William Laslie	27.12.1843	£16 15 0
1.10.1802	James Elliott	James	Blacksmith	Newcastle	William Laslie		
30.11.1802	Mark Heaton	William	Husbandman	Felling Shore, Durham	Alexander Doeg		
30.11.1802	Richard Sharp	Richard	Pilot	Felling Shore, Durham			
20.12.1802	Edward Charlton	Charles	Gentleman	Newcastle	Alexander Doeg	25.6.1827	£10 1 6
22.10.1802	John Brown	Cuthbert	Keelman	Ouseburn	Henry Charlton		
2.3.1803	Jacob Hall	George	Mariner	Ballast Hills	Henry Wright		
27.7.1803	Wm Wilson	William	Mariner (decd)	Ballast Hills	Henry Wright		
15.7.1803	William Forbes	William	Labourer	Sandgate	Henry Wright		
15.7.1803	Martin Spoors	John	Glassmaker	East Ballast Hills	George Young		
15.7.1803	John Gibson	William	Shipwright	East Ballast Hills	George Young		
25.7.1803	Stephen Ridley	John	Master Mariner	North Shore	George Young	5.10.1812	£2 12 2
22.10.1803	Thomas Young	Cuthbert	Shipwright	South Shields, Durham	George Young		
10.12.1803	James Kinlock	Alexander	Gent	Newcastle	John Bell	24.6.1813	£2 12 2
21.5.1804	John Brown	Leonard	Pilot	Wallsend	Alexander Doeg		
28.3.1804	David Rennoldson	John	Shipwright	North Shore	Henry Wright	5.10.1812	£2 12 2
23.5.1803	Thomas Urron	William	Drayman	Sandgate	His father		
23.5.1803	James Dixon	Matthew	Miller	Barras Bridge, Newcastle	Robert Gothard		
19.4.1803	Richard Armour	Peter	Master Mariner	Sandgate	Robert Gothard		

Date of indenture	Name of apprentice	Christian name of Father	Occupation of Father	Place of origin	Shipwright to whom apprenticed	Date of freedom	Price for freedom
25.8.1804	John Gibson	John	Brazier	North Shields	Henry Wright	28.12.1812	£2 12 4
13.7.1804	Robert Smith	John	Mariner	South Shields	John Bell		
7.7.1804	James Gunn	William	Labourer	Sandgate	Robert Gothard		
30.7.1804	Henry Brownlee	Henry	Keelman	Sandgate	Robert Gothard		
1.10.1804	George Todd	Thomas	Labourer	Dents Hole	William Laslie		
22.8.1804	John Barker	Anthony		Ballast Hills	William Carss		
15.12.1804	Thomas Bulmer	Richard	Shipbuilder	South Shields	John Bell		
10.10.1804	Thomas Alexander	William	Shipwright	North Shore	John Rennoldson		
20.8.1806	George Laing	Geo.	Mariner	North Shore	Robert Gothard		
26.12.1806	George Harrison			Newcastle	William Laslie		
25.5.1807	Bartholomew Birtley	Cuthbert	Keelman	Ouseburn	Henry Wright		
31.8.1807	John Capstaff	John	Glassmaker	North Shore	Henry Charlton		
17.7.1807	Robert Jubb	Christopher		South Shields	Thomas Forsyth		
28.12.1807	John George Bruce			South Shields	Henry Wright		
10.5.1808	Matthew Brown	Jonathan	Shipwright	South Shore, Durham	Joseph Coxon	*	
23.6.1808	Charles Martindale			Jarrow	Simon Temple		
17.8.1808	Thomas Bell	John	Waterman	North Shore	James Carse		
20.6.1808	James Carse			South Shields	Henry Wright		
20.4.1809	Ralph Mood	Ralph		West Ballast Hills	William Wright		
24.4.1809	Angus McKenzie Anderson	Andrew		North Shore	William Wright		
11.4.1809	Matthew Nichols	Thomas		Ballast Hills	William Wright		
20.5.1809	Thomas Cookson			West Boldon, Durham	Simon Temple		
20.11.1809	Robert Gibson	William	Yeoman	Newcastle	William Laslie		
31.3.1810	Roger Hopper	Roger	Yeoman	Howdon Pans	Simon Temple		
31.3.1810	Hugh Hume			Howdon Pans	Simon Temple		

Date of indenture	Name of apprentice	Christian name of Father	Occupation of Father	Place of origin	Shipwright to whom apprenticed	Date of freedom	Price for freedom
31.3.1810	Charles Borthwick		Yeoman	Howdon Pans	Simon Temple		
31.3.1810	Thomas Maffon		Yeoman	Jarrow	Simon Temple		
31.3.1810	John Smith			North Shields	Simon Temple		
31.3.1810	John Borston		Yeoman	Howdon Pans	Simon Temple		
31.3.1810	William Gordon	James	Shipwright	Howdon Pans	Simon Temple		
17.4.1810	Robert Harkis	Robert	Carpenter	South Shields	Henry Wright		
28.4.1810	Thomas Coats	Thomas	Yeoman	Newcastle	Matthew Henderson		
29.9.1810	Archibald Irwin	Tho.	Shoemaker	Sandgate	William Carss		
19.2.1810	Wm Davidson	Wm	Master Mariner	New Road, Newcastle			
29.9.1810	Matthew James	Wm		Sandgate	William Carss		
27.9.1810	Thomas Rutter	Tho.		Ballast Hills	William Carss		
27.3.1810	Edward Trewhitt Hall	Miles	Shipwright	Newcastle	Wm Wright		
20.3.1810	Stephen Donkin	Stephen	Keelman	Newcastle	William Laslie		
10.10.1810	Ephraim Gilchrist	John	Pilot	Saint Anthony's	William Laslie		
24.1.1812	John Armstrong	Thomas	Mariner	North Shields	William Laslie		
14.3.1811	John Petrie			Newcastle	William Carss		
22.3.1811	James Eddey	Wm	Wherryman	Newcastle	Alexander Doeg		
11.4.1811	John Doeg	Stephen	Mariner	North Shore	Alexander Doeg	24.6.1846	£3 8 0
[?].1811	Joseph Morrison	David		North Shore	Alexander Doeg		
6.6.1811	James Miller	James	Potter	Newcastle	Alexander Doeg		
28.5.1811	Wm Temple				Wm Carss		
28.5.1811	Thomas Laws	Benj'n	Waterman	North Shore	Wm Carss		
22.4.1811	Ambrose Hopper	Ambrose		Ballast Hills	Wm Wright	4.10.1824	£5 9 6
15.6.1811	Nathaniel Graham Anderson	John	Tailor	South Shields	Thomas Forsyth		
15.5.1811	John Blair	Wm	Farmer	Jesmond	Thomas Forsyth		

275

Date of indenture	Name of apprentice	Christian name of Father	Occupation of Father	Place of origin	Shipwright to whom apprenticed	Date of freedom	Price for freedom
4.4.1811	Geo. Hunter	Geo.		South Shields	Thomas Forsyth		
27.5.1812	Thomas Menham			Newcastle	Alexander Doeg		
11.2.1812	Robert Smith	Thomas	Master Mariner	North Shields	Thomas Forsyth		
15.10.1812	George Clark Smith	Alexander	Mariner (decd)	South Shields			
26.12.1811	Matthew Moffett	William		South Shields	Thomas Forsyth		
13.2.1813	William Dodds	Eleanor (widow)		South Shields	Henry Wright		
20.3.1813	Peter Vinton		Mariner	South Shields	Henry Wright		
25.9.1813	Thomas Vint	Thomas	Shoemaker	South Shields	Thomas Forsyth		
25.5.1813	James Taylor	George	Shipwright	South Shields	Thomas Forsyth		
5.8.1813	George Gordon Waddell		Glassfounder	Gateshead	Thomas Forsyth		
25.9.1813	John Smith	John	Cartwright	South Shields	William Laslie		
15.9.1813	Stoddard Baird	Matthew		North Shore	Thomas Forsyth		
25.8.1813	Thomas Clennel			St Peters Quay	Alexander Doeg	*	
7.4.1814	Thomas Doeg	John	Mariner	Newcastle	Alexander Doeg	*	
3.11.1812	George Fleck	Thomas	Mariner	Sandgate	Alexander Doeg		
11.4.1814	Nicholas Wilkie	George			Alexander Doeg		
2.6.1814	Thomas Bell	James	Master Mariner	South Shields	Thomas Forsyth	11.10.1821	
14.8.1813	William Scott	Thomas	Yeoman	Sandyford	Alexander Doeg		
26.4.1814	Matthew Grey	William		North Shore	Alexander Doeg	*	
11.1.1815	George Arnison	Henry		South Shields	Henry Wright		
24.6.1815	George Sadler	Matthew		Dunston, Durham	Thomas Sadler		
5.6.1815	John Bainbridge	Robert	Waterman	Dunston, Durham	Thomas Sadler	3.10.1825	£4 3 6
3.6.1815	Isaac Pollock	Timothy	Gardener	Rosehill	Wm Wright		

Date of indenture	Name of apprentice	Christian name of Father	Occupation of Father	Place of origin	Shipwright to whom apprenticed	Date of freedom	Price for freedom
4.3.1816	Lancelot Bulman	George	Roper	City of London	Thomas Sadler		
13.10.1816	John Taylor	John	Innkeeper	South Shields	Thomas Forsyth	27.12.1842	
1.4.1818	James Young	James		South Shields	Thomas Young		
28.3.1821	Christopher Stephenson						
16.6.1821	Robt Gibson	James	Shipwright	Newcastle	Joseph Farrington		
25.8.1821	William Newton	John	Shipowner	South Shields	Thomas Young		
15.4.1822	Richard Hansell Bell	Robert	Keelman	Dunston, Durham	Thomas Sadler		
13.4.1822	Henry Thew	Sarah	(Widow)	South Shields	Thomas Forsyth		
26.8.1822	Thompson Smith	Christopher	Shipowner	East Boldon, Durham	Thomas Young	28.12.1829	
11.9.1822	William Soulsley Stephenson	Charles	Merchant	Newcastle	Joseph Farrington		
30.10.1822	George Wilson	James	Weaver	East Ballast Hills	Joseph Farrington		
28.1.1823	William Smith	William	Cordwainer	East Ballast Hills	Joseph Farrington		
30.5.1823	Robert Jones	Shadrack	Shipwright	North Shields	William Smith		
9.8.1823	Edward Shepherd	John	Sawyer	North Shields	William Smith		
6.10.1823	Thomas Clemention	Richard	Quarryman	North Shields	William Smith		
6.10.1823	Robert Sadler	Jeremiah	Keelman	Dunston, Durham	Thomas Sadler		
3.11.1823	Francis Booth	Matthew		Dunston, Durham	Thomas Sadler		
6.2.1824	William Wright	Eleanor	(Widow)	South Shields	Thomas Forsyth		
10.3.1824	Thomas Thew	William	Shipowner	South Shields	Thomas Young		
9.2.1824	Thomas Crow	Robert	Master	South Shields	Thomas Young		
9.2.1824	William Gray	Lambert	Mariner	North Shields	Wm Smith		
23.2.1824	Edward Henderson	Henry		North Shields	Wm Smith		
23.3.1824	Robert Bailey	Robert		North Shields	Wm Smith		

Date of indenture	Name of apprentice	Christian name of Father	Occupation of Father	Place of origin	Shipwright to whom apprenticed	Date of freedom	Price for freedom
12.6.1824	John Nixon	James	Grocer	South Shields	Thomas Young		
17.9.1824	Lancelot Bell	Lancelot	Smith	St Peters, Newcastle	Wm Smith		
29.9.1824	Thos. Bennett	Margaret	(Widow)	South Shields	Thos. Forsyth		
26.5.1824	John Fraser		Yeoman	Tynemouth	William Smith		
24.5.1824	Ephraim Fenwick	Ephraim	Waggonman	Lamesley, Durham	Joseph Farrington		
4.10.1824	Thos. Hill	Willm	Cartman	Byker Bar	Ambrose Hopper		
26.11.1824	Martin Morris	John	Master Mariner	North Shields	Thomas Forsyth		
11.1.1825	William Hall Maddison	John	Upholsterer	Newcastle	William Wright		
22.1.1825	William Taylor	Matthew	Shipwright	Ouseburn	William Wright		
11.1.1825	Joseph Howe	Joseph	Mason	North Shore	Ambrose Hopper		
8.2.1825	James Cuthbertson	John Cook	Mariner	Tynemouth	William Smith		
6.4.1825	Adam Winls	John	Shipwright	St Lawrence, Newcastle	William Smith		
16.5.1825	William Wilds	Ralph	Shipwright	South Shields	Thomas Young		
29.12.1824	Thomas Willis	Catherine	(Widow)	North Shore	Joseph Farrington		
29.12.1824	Robert Fairs	Margaret	(Widow)	North Shore	Joseph Farrington		
29.9.1825	James Patterson Wright	James	Soapmaker	Newcastle	William Wright		
25.10.1825	Joseph Man	Joseph	Mariner	Newcastle	Joseph Farrington		
15.11.1825	William Thomas Couper	Lancelot	Farmer	Willington, Durham	Thomas Young		
29.4.1826	Thomas Sharer	Thomas	Gent	South Shields	James Evans	*	
29.4.1826	George Sharer	Thomas	Gent	South Shields	James Evans	*	

Date of indenture	Name of apprentice	Christian name of Father	Occupation of Father	Place of origin	Shipwright to whom apprenticed	Date of freedom	Price for freedom
14.5.1827	James Whittle	James	Shipwright	North Shields	Willm Smith		
7.6.1827	John Gibson	George	Shipowner	South Shields	Thomas Young		
18.10.1827	William Carter	John	Shipwright	St Peter's Quay	William Smith		
16.1.1828	Martin Taylor	Matthew	Carpenter	North Shore	Ambrose Hopper		
16.1.1828	Matthew Taylor	Matthew	Carpenter	North Shore	Ambrose Hopper		
1.3.1828	Thomas Brown	Robert	Shipwright	North Shields	Wm Smith		
4.2.1828	Thomas Purvis	John	Master Mariner	South Shields	Thos. Forsyth		
9.2.1828	Isaac Milburn			Dunston, Durham	Thos. Sadler		
27.6.1827	John Bowlt	John		Bill Quay, Durham	Rich'd Sharp		
25.4.1828	George Cunningham	Elizabeth	(Widow)	North Shore	Wm Wright		
17.5.1828	John Ness Coxon	Edwd	Shipowner	Wethoe, Durham	Thos. Forsyth		
26.11.1828	Robert White	John	Master Mariner	North Shields	Wm Smith		
18.4.1829	Luke Gray	Mary	(Widow)	North Shields	Wm Smith		
23.5.1829	James Houze King	Rich'd	Shoemaker	North Shields	Thos. Young		
24.2.1830	William Whittle	James	Shipwright	North Shields	Willm Smith		
9.3.1830	James Gunn	Isabella	(Widow)	North Shields	Willm Smith		
22.3.1830	William Ward	William	Boatbuilder	South Shields	Thos. Forsyth		
29.3.1830	John Simpson	John	Tummer	North Shields	William Smith		
10.8.1830	George Hunter	George	Shipwright	North Shore	William Wright		
25.9.1830	John Snaith	William	Shipwright	South Shields	Thomas Forsyth		
28.6.1830	Edward Johnson	Patrick	Shipwright	Dents Hole	William Smith		
5.7.1830	William Anderson	Thomas	Master Mariner	South Shields	Thompson Smith	*	
7.7.1830	John Ogilvy	James	Merchant	City of Westminster	Thompson Smith		

Date of indenture	Name of apprentice	Christian name of Father	Occupation of Father	Place of origin	Shipwright to whom apprenticed	Date of freedom	Price for freedom
4.9.1830	Francis Bainbridge	Ann	(Widow)	Dunston, Durham	Thomas Sadler		
25.10.1830	William Towell	William		North Shields	William Smith		
20.1.1831	William Renshaw	George		Ballast Hills	William Wright		
21.3.1831	Thomas Alexander Trotter	Andrew		North Shields	Thompson Smith	*	
9.3.1831	John Watson Smith	William		Dunston	Thomas Sadler		
25.5.1831	Thomas Webster	Alexander	Shipwright	St Peter's Quay	William Smith		
6.6.1831	Matthew Hardy	Matthew	Cordwainer	St Peter's Quay	William Smith		
26.9.1831	Robert Dixon Taylor	James	Shipwright	Ballast Hills	William Wright		
4.11.1832	John Carter	Mary	(Widow)	Newcastle	William Smith		
16.1.1832	William Havery	Wm	Shipwright	North Shields	William Smith		
16.5.1832	Robert Royal	William	Master Mariner	North Shields	William Smith		
6.8.1832	Christian Ker Spence	William Whitaker	Draper	All Saints, Newcastle	William Wright	27.12.1840	£3 1 0
9.4.1833	Frederick Brown	Elizabeth	(Widow)	Ouseburn	William Wright		
21.5.1833	Thomas Harding Dixon	John	Mariner	Tynemouth	William Smith		
25.9.1833	Robert Waddle	Thomas	Mariner	Tynemouth	William Smith		
6.7.1833	Ambrose Hopper	Thomas	Founder (decd)	North Shore	Ambrose Hopper (his uncle)		
22.10.1833	James Stephens	William	Shipowner	North Shields	William Smith		
4.11.1833	John Porter	Robert	Mariner	North Shields	William Smith		
12.11.1833	John Gray	John	Mariner	North Shields	William Smith		
19.9.1833	Stephen Caverhill	David	Mariner	Sandgate	Ambrose Hopper		
21.1.1834	John Hall	John	Keelman	Pandon	Ambrose Hopper	29.12.1845	£4 10 0

Date of indenture	Name of apprentice	Christian name of Father	Occupation of Father	Place of origin	Shipwright to whom apprenticed	Date of freedom	Price for freedom
2.1.1834	Robert Armstrong	Nicholas	Shipowner	St Andrews, Newcastle	William Wright		
21.5.1834	Robert Grey	Robert	Mariner	North Shields	William Smith		
6.6.1834	John Lupton	Isaac	Shipwright	North Shields	William Smith		
19.9.1834	Ralph Walter Liddell	Thomas	Husbandman	North Shields	William Smith		
24.9.1834	Edward Robinson	William	Master Mariner	St Peters Quay	William Smith		
10.10.1834	George Gair	George	Hostler	Tynemouth	William Smith		
23.10.1834	Thomas Nelson	Thomas	Common Brewer	South Shields	William Smith		
30.9.1839	Thomas Hopper	Thomas	Founder (decd)	North Shore	Thomas Young		
3.2.1841	Martin Jackson Morris	Martin	Shipowner	North Shields	Ambrose Hopper		
5.5.1842	Robinson Wilson	William	Shipowner (decd)	Blyth	William Smith		
26.7.1842	Thomas Metcalfe	Thomas	Esquire	West Boldon, Durham	William Smith		
26.12.1840	William Edward Boutland	William	Shipbuilder	Bill Quay, Durham	Thompson Smith		
14.6.1844	Richard Smith Hopper Hopper	Ambrose	Shipwright	North Shore	John Christopher Morris	29.12.1845	£2 16 0
14.6.1844	William Brown	Richard	Shipwright	North Shore	His father	25.6.1849	£2 10 0
28.12.1846	John George Boutland	William	Shipwright	Bill Quay	Ambrose Hopper		
28.12.1846	Edward Pringle Boutland	William	Shipwright	Bill Quay	J. C. Morris		
27.9.1847	Thomas Metcalfe	George	Shipwright	North Shields	William Edward Boutland / John Taylor		

Date of indenture	Name of apprentice	Christian name of Father	Occupation of Father	Place of origin	Shipwright to whom apprenticed	Date of freedom	Price for freedom
27.9.1847	William Sanderson	William	Master Mariner (decd)				
13.10.1849	Robert Pringle Boutland	William	Shipwright	South Shields	John Taylor		
[?c.1837]	David Morris	John Christopher	Shipwright	Bill Quay	W. E. Boutland		
6.5.1855	James Pashley	Isabella	(Widow)	St Lawrence, Newcastle	His father	27.12.1850	£4 18 0
6.11.1855	Thomas Hutchinson Hopper	Ambrose	Shipwright	Newcastle	Ambrose & Richard Hopper	27.12.1864	£3 6 0
30.9.1854	Robert Carter	Robert	Shipwright	Bill Quay	John & David Morris	26.12.1907	£2 10 0
30.9.1854	Thomas Carter	William	Shipwright	Bill Quay	John & David Morris		
22.10.1854	Robert Bell Harrison	Robert	Shipwright	St Lawrence, Newcastle	John & David Morris		
16.4.1851	James Gardner Taylor	John	Shipwright	North Shore	Ambrose & Richard Hopper	26.12.1872	£6 16 0
18.11.1856	Thomas Lawson	Edward	Farmer	Hebburn, Blue House, Durham	J. & D. Morris		

Date of indenture	Name of apprentice	Christian name of Father	Occupation of Father	Place of origin	Shipwright to whom apprenticed	Date of freedom	Price for freedom
[c.1838?]	John Morris	John Christopher			His father	14.4.1857	£7 6 0
17.4.1857	John Carter	William	Shipwright	St Lawrence, Bill Quay	J. & D. Morris		
8.2.1860	Charles Morris Carter	Robert Young	Shipwright	Pelaw Main, Durham	J. & D. Morris	26.12.1908	£2 10 0
[c.1837?]	Richard Hopper	Ambrose	Shipwright	Newcastle	William Wright	25.4.1864	£10 18 0
[c.1837?]	Henry Penman	Andrew	Shipwright	Dunston	William Smith	25.4.1864	£10 18 0

(B) Members of the Company by Patrimony

Date entered	Name	Father's Christian name	Date of freedom	Paid for freedom
6.3.1647	Peter Turner	Geo.		
29.9.1659	Tho. Atkinson	Nicholas		
27.12.1660	Robert Lowson	Willm		
27.12.1662	James Ogle	John		
9.6.1663	John Otway	Tho.		
27.12.1664	Mathew Reed	Mathew		
29.9.1665	Charles Bowman	Christopher		
27.12.1665	Edward Wilson	Edward (decd)	1.12.1673	
24.5.1670	John Hunter	Cuthbert		
2.2.1671	Stephen Ellet			
2.2.1671	Joshua Ellet			
27.12.1671	Joseph Harle	Charles		
27.12.1671	Nathaniell Harle	Charles		
27.12.1671	Jonathan Harle	Charles		
27.12.1671	Josiah Harle	Charles		
2.2.1672	Robert Rogers	Francis		
2.2.1672	Josias Selby	George		
9.4.1672	George Tailor	George	28.12.1685	£2 2 2
9.4.1672	John Tailor	George	21.12.1691	£2 2 2
13.2.1673	William Wilkinson	Robert		
1.4.1673	George Shevill	William		
1.4.1673	Lancelot Turner	Peter		
20.6.1673	John Briggs	Robert		
27.12.1673	Robert Durham	George	2.2.1674	£2 2 2
	Thomas Tailor	George		
25.4.1674	John Middleton	Leonard		
25.4.1674	William Cooke	John		

Date entered	Name	Father's Christian name	Date of freedom	Paid for freedom
24.6.1674	William Colyer	Heugh		
24.6.1674	James Colyer	Heugh		
29.9.1674	Raiph Wilson	Richard		
29.9.1674	Stephen Brewhouse	Stephen		
28.12.1674	Jason Turner	John	25.7.1689	
	Charles Steele	Roger	20.1.1676	£2 2 8
	Thomas Forster	Cuthbert	16.5.1676	£2 2 2
	Robert Beckwith	George	29.9.1676	£2 2 2
	Thomas Nicholson	John	27.12.1677	£2 2 2
	John Snowball		27.12.1677	£2 2 2
	Peter Dawson		2.4.1678	£2 2 2
	Jeremiah Cooke		2.4.1678	£2 2 2
	John Arrowsmith		27.12.1678	£2 2 2
	Daniel Lawson		27.12.1678	£2 2 2
	John Kirkeley		27.12.1678	£2 9 9
	Cuthbert Forster		24.6.1679	£2 2 2
29.9.1680	John Spurne	Thomas	26.4.1698	£2 2 2
29.9.1680	Thomas Spurne	Thomas	26.4.1683	£2 2 4
18.4.1682	John Wilkinson	John	27.12.1695	£2 2 4
	Edward Greene	Luke	29.3.1687	£7 9 8
27.12.1686	Richard Cooke	Anthony		
	Thomas Wilkinson	Robert		
20.12.1688	Roger Jobling	Cuthbert	24.6.1696	£2 2 2
2.4.1689	John Bone		1.10.1689	£3 2 2
	Thomas Burrell		19.1.1691	£2 2 8
	Edward Wilkinson		24.6.1691	£2 2 2
	John Taylor		24.6.1691	£2 2 2
	John Smith		21.12.1691	£2 2 2
	Matthew Taylor	John		

Date entered	Name	Father's Christian name	Date of freedom	Paid for freedom
	Robt Hoxton		21.12.1691	£2 2 2
	Robt Simpson		21.12.1691	£2 2 2
	Wm Cook	John	21.12.1691	£2 2 2
	Wm Cook	Wm	21.12.1691	£2 2 2
27.12.1692	Roger Atkinson	John		
27.12.1692	John Trewhitt	John	26.4.1698	£2 2 2
27.12.1692	William Trewhitt	John	free n.d.	
	John Atkinson	John	29.9.1693	£2 2 2
	Thomas Wrangham		27.12.1694	£2 11 2
	Robt Forster		18.10.1695	£2 2 2
	John Boutiman		27.12.1695	£2 2 2
	James Wilkinson		27.12.1695	£2 2 2
27.12.1695	Robert Chaitor	Wm	22.3.1715	£2 9 2
24.6.1696	Edward Wilson	Edward		
28.12.1696	Thomas Dixon	Thomas		
28.12.1696	Wm Foxton	Thomas		
	Peter Forster		6.4.1697	£2 2 2
	George Kirkley		26.4.1698	£2 2 2
	John Beckwith		26.4.1698	£2 2 0
	Roger Otway		29.9.1698	£2 2 2
	Edward Burrell		29.9.1698	£2 7 2
	Henry Wallas		30.10.1698	£2 2 2
18.11.1698	Thomas Forster	Thomas	27.12.1698	£2 2 2
	Wm Wrangham		11.4.1699	£2 2 0
	Thos. Wallas	Thomas	11.4.1699	£2 2 0
	Thos. Reed	Wm		
24.6.1699	Cuthbert Strother			
	Wm Park	Wm	21.10.1699	£2 2 2
	Robt Kirkley		2.4.1700	£2 2 6

Date entered	Name	Father's Christian name	Date of freedom	Paid for freedom
29.12.1700	John Nicholson	Richard	22.4.1701	£2 2 2
	Robt Thackery		22.4.1701	£2 2 2
	James Wallas		29.9.1701	£2 2 2
	Wm Shew			
27.12.1701	Francis Burden	Francis	8.10.1722	£2 2 2
27.12.1701	Peter Lawson	Daniel	30.3.1703	£2 2 2
28.12.1702	John Waite	Peter	30.3.1703	£2 2 2
	Robert Stokoe		24.12.1710	£2 2 8
27.12.1703	John Snowball	John	18.4.1704	£2 2 2
	Thomas Hopper	Cuthbert	29.9.1704	£2 2 2
	Henry Fletcher		27.12.1704	£2 2 2
	Thomas Parker		27.12.1704	£2 2 2
	Ralph Wilkin		27.12.1704	£2 2 2
	Wm Hoxton		27.12.1704	£2 2 2
	James Forster		6.1.1705	£2 2 2
	John Milbourne		29.9.1705	£2 10 10
	James Reed		27.12.1705	£2 2 2
	John Kipling		27.12.1705	£2 2 2
	Benjamin Gibson		27.12.1705	£2 2 2
	John Hall		27.12.1705	£2 2 2
	Edward Forster		16.2.1706	£2 2 2
	Wm Wilson		26.3.1706	£2 2 2
	Wm Robinson			£2 2 2
	Robert Trewhitt			£2 2 2
30.9.1706	Peter Waite	Peter	24.6.1708	£2 2 2
	Wm Wilkinson		21.12.1708	£2 2 2
	Avera Trewhitt			
21.12.1708	Francis Waite	Peter	25.12.1708	£2 2 2
	Richard Kipling	John		

287

Date entered	Name	Father's Christian name	Date of freedom	Paid for freedom
[?]1709	John Burrell	Edward	11.7.1726	£2 2 2
	John Wilkinson		26.4.1709	£2 2 2
	Robert Atkinson		29.9.1709	£2 2 2
	James Trewhitt		29.9.1709	£2 3 2
	Joseph Barber		29.9.1709	£2 2 2
	Willowby Hall		21.12.1709	£2 2 2
	Richard Urwen		2.1.1710	£2 2 2
	John Trewhitt	John	27.12.1710	£2 2 8
	Henry Robinson	Gawin	4.2.1711	£2 2 2
	John Park	John	31.3.1711	£2 4 2
	William Cary		25.6.1711	£2 2 2
	Thomas Wilson	George	24.12.1711	£2 2 2
	Richard Trewhitt	Robert	24.12.1711	£2 2 2
7.4.1713	Ralph Waite	Peter		
7.4.1713	Ralph Lowson	James	30.9.1723	£2 2 2
	Cuthbert Preston	Edward	26.12.1713	£2 2 8
	Ralph Wilson	John	30.3.1714	£2 2 2
	Wm Unthank	John	8.4.1714	£2 2 2
	John Taylor	George	13.4.1714	£2 4 2
	Mark Coxon	Archibald	13.4.1714	£2 2 8
	Thomas Dixon	Gilbert	24.6.1714	£2 2 2
	John Trewhitt	Averah	8.9.1714	£2 2 2
	Thomas Potter	William	8.9.1714	£2 2 2
	Thomas Taylor	George	27.12.1714	£2 2 2
	John James	Henry	27.12.1714	£2 3 2
	Geo. Gordon	John	27.12.1714	£2 6 5
	Edward Park	William	24.6.1715	£2 17 8
	George Wilson	George	29.9.1715	£2 4 8
	Wm Glen	James	27.12.1715	£3 1 2

Date entered	Name	Father's Christian name	Date of freedom	Paid for freedom
	John Reed	Thomas	3.4.1716	£2 19 8
	Robert Wallas	John	29.9.1716	£2 4 8
[?]1717	John Rennoldson	Wm	29.9.1744	£2 12 2
	Wm Barber	Thomas	27.12.1717	£2 4 8
	Wm Trumble	Wm	27.12.1717	£2 2 2
	Thomas Fletcher	Wm	29.9.1718	£3 2 2
	Thomas Wrangham	Thomas	27.12.1718	£2 4 8
	Henry Dawson	Richard	31.3.1719	£2 7 2
	Cuthbert Forster	Cuthbert	31.3.1719	£3 2 2
	Robert Briggs	John	11.4.1720	£2 6 2
	John Hume	John	2.10.1720	£2 15 10
	Ralph Thew	Wm	27.3.1722	£2 2 2
	Roger Cowen	Thomas	30.3.1722	£4 7 2
	John Coxon	Archibald	29.9.1722	£2 2 8

[At about this time entries of freemen's sons in the register of indentures ceased, but for a number of years until about 1786 a number of them were recorded in the index to the register, although without any date. The following are those for whom there is no record of their having become free shipwrights.]

John Bryden	John	
Robert Coxon	John	
George Cram	George	
Thomas Donkin	William	
Ralph Fisher	Jacob	
Ralph Hall	Ralph	
Andrew Hall	Ralph	
Joseph Hall	Ralph	
William Hall	Ralph	
Matthew Hall	Ralph	
Michael Johnson	John	
William Maughlin	George	

Date entered	Name	Father's Christian name	Date of freedom	Paid for freedom
	John Maughling	George		
	John Park	John		
	Cuthbert Pearson	William		
	William Pearson	William		
	William Trewhitt	Francis		
	Edward Trewhitt	Francis		
	Thomas Wilson	Robert		
	John Wilson	Robert		
	George Wilson	Robert		
	Thomas Wilson	Thomas		
	William Wilson	Thomas		
	Peter Forster	Peter	24.6.1723	£2 2 2
	Edward Trewhitt	William	24.6.1723	£2 2 2
	Robert Dixon	Gilbert	8.8.1723	£2 2 2
	Ralph Reed	Wm	30.9.1723	£2 2 2
	John Snowball	George	6.1.1724	£2 3 2
	Joshua Farmer	Peter	7.4.1724	£2 2 2
	George Tulip	Samuel	9.12.1724	£2 15 6
	Thomas Wilson	Richard	24.6.1725	£2 12 2
	John Trewhitt	William	27.12.1725	£2 12 2
	Robert Cay	Henry	11.7.1726	£2 4 2
	Robert Wallis	Thomas	27.12.1726	£2 12 2
	John Emmerson	George	16.6.1727	£3 0 8
	Thomas Wallis	Thomas	4.9.1727	£2 12 2
	Robert Fletcher	Henry	21.12.1727	£2 17 2
	William Snowball	George	27.12.1727	£2 12 2
	William Tulip	Samuel	27.12.1727	£2 12 2
	Joseph Edgar	Robert	27.12.1727	£2 12 8

Date entered	Name	Father's Christian name	Date of freedom	Paid for freedom
	Edward Durham	Robert	8.4.1728	£2 12 2
	Thomas Forster	Thomas	1.10.1728	£2 12 2
	Robert Collingwood	Robert	1.10.1728	£2 12 2
	John Beckwith	John	27.12.1728	£2 12 8
	John Hoxton	Robert	29.9.1729	£2 12 2
	Wm Hanby	Wm	29.9.1729	£2 12 2
	John Edgar	Robert	27.12.1729	£2 12 2
	Amram Maughlin	George	25.6.1733	£2 12 2
	David Hudson	Richard	16.4.1734	£2 15 2
	Luke Younghusband	Richard	27.12.1734	£2 12 2
	Wm Rennison	Wm	15.1.1735	£2 12 2
	Fenwick Bone	John	25.2.1735	£2 12 2
	Wm Charleton	John	29.9.1735	£0 10 0*
	Thos. Robinson		29.9.1736	£2 12 0
	William Park	Wm	24.6.1737	£2 12 0
	Wm Wilkinson	William	27.12.1737	£2 12 0
	Thomas Cay	Henry	4.4.1738	£2 12 2
	George Fletcher	Henry	29.9.1738	£2 17 2
	John Thackwray	Robert	29.9.1738	£2 13 8
	Thomas Taylor	John	6.1.1739	£2 12 2
	Enoch White	James	16.1.1739	£2 12 2
	Paul Park	Wm	11.9.1739	£2 14 8
	Thomas Wilson	William	16.4.1739	£2 12 2
	Thomas Baird	Thomas	16.4.1739	£2 12 2
	Thomas Slater	Edward	29.9.1740	£2 12 2
	George Guy	Robert	20.10.1740	£2 12 2

* "Wm Charleton, son of John Charleton, shipwright, was this day admitted to his freedom of the Company and paid for the same towards building the meeting house (10/–), the Company in regard to his misfortune of loosing [sic] his foot and being very poor abating him the rest of his fees. 24.6.1738   The above named William Charleton this day paid into the Company the further sum of £2 2s. which with 10s. above mentioned is the full sum paid upon the admission of any freeman."

291

Date entered	Name	Father's Christian name	Date of freedom	Paid for freedom
29.9.1741	Archibald Coxon	Mark	31.3.1741	£2 12 2
29.9.1741	John Wall	Bryan		
	Bryan Wall	Bryan	29.9.1750	£2 12 2
	Francis Trewhitt	Wm	20.4.1742	£2 12 2
	John Headlam	John	3.2.1743	£6 12 2
	Leighton Preston	Cuthbert	18.10.1743	£2 12 2
	James White	James	10.10.1744	£2 12 2
	Robert Wilson	Robert	16.4.1745	£2 14 2
	Robert French	Jonathan	30.9.1745	£2 13 2
28.12.1747	Wm Wilkinson	William jun.		
	Wm Hindmarsh	George	18.4.1749	£2 14 8
	George Liddell	Robert	3.7.1749	£2 13 2
	Edward Wilkinson	Wm	29.4.1749	£2 12 2
	George Rennison [Rennoldson]	Wm	29.4.1749	£2 13 2
	John Park	Edward	29.4.1749	£2 14 8
	George Mow	John	29.4.1749	£2 12 8
	Robert Thompson	Wm	6.1.1750	£3 1 2
	John Coxon	John	6.1.1750	£2 15 8
	Ralph Hall	John	29.9.1750	£3 2 8
	Joseph Taylor	John		£2 17 2
[?]1750	Wm Henderson	Wm	27.12.1755	£2 17 2
[?]1751	Joseph Rennoldson	John		
27.12.1751	Henry Stainsby	Henry	21.10.1751	£3 12 2
	John Burrell	John	29.12.1758	£3 6 2
	John Taylor	Thomas	31.3.1752	£3 0 2
	John Semple	John	25.6.1753	£2 12 2
	Edward Wilkinson	Edward	20.4.1756	£2 14 8
	William Thowburn	John	27.1.1757	£2 19 8

Date entered	Name	Father's Christian name	Date of freedom	Paid for freedom
	George Maughling	Amram	27.12.1757	£2 13 2
[?]1757	John Rennoldson	John	29.12.1758	£2 19 2
29.12.1758	Lionel Robson	Lionel	29.12.1758	£3 6 2
	Thomas Taylor	Thomas	20.4.1759	£3 12 2
	Thomas Emmerson Headlam	John		
[?]1760	John Hall	Ralph	24.6.1760	£3 0 2
	John Lettiney	John	29.9.1764	£3 8 2
	John Eyons	James	12.1.1773	£4 4 6
	Robert Mackintosh	Michael		
[?]1778	William Wilson	Robert		
[?]1784	Thomas Taylor	Thomas	27.12.1785	£2 16 2
	David Rennoldson	John	27.12.1785	£2 16 2
	Alexander Doag [Doeg]	Henry	2.10.1786	£4 0 2
	William Curry	Ephraim	27.12.1787	£2 12 2
	Robert Gothard	John		
28.12.1795	Charles Charlton	Henry	24.6.1801	£3 8 2
	Wm Carss	Wm	28.12.1801	£2 12 2
	Joseph Brown	Joseph	20.4.1802	£5 0 0
	George Cram	George	27.12.1815	£2 12 2
5.10.1812	James Evans	James	16.4.1816	£2 12 2
	Thomas Forsyth	Thomas	6.10.1817	£5 0 0
	William Wilson	Robert	24.6.1822	£2 17 6
	William Wilson	William	27.12.1824	£3 13 0
	William Wright jun.	Henry	27.12.1831	£4 0 0
	John Wright	Henry	27.12.1875	£2 18 0
	William Boutland Morris	David	26.12.1876	£2 10 0
	John Christopher Charles Morris	David	27.12.1879	£2 10 0
	David Charles Morris	David	26.12.1888	£2 10 0
	Robert Bell Harrison	Robert Bell		

Date entered	Name	Father's Christian name	Date of freedom	Paid for freedom
	Henry Hunter Doeg	John	6.5.1893	£2 10 0
	John Stephen Doeg	John	26.12.1896	£2 10 0
	James Johnson Harrison	Robert Bell	26.12.1898	£2 10 0
	John Colling Boutland	Robert Pringle	26.12.1900	£2 10 0
	John Boutland	John George	26.12.1904	£2 10 0
	David Morris	David Charles	26.12.1904	£2 10 0
	James Everett Hopper	Richard	26.12.1908	£2 10 0
	Alfred Carter	Robert	26.12.1908	£2 10 0
	Robert Pringle Boutland	John Colling	27.12.1909	£2 10 0
	John George Boutland	John	26.12.1914	£2 10 0
	Allan Hunter Doeg	Henry Hunter	26.12.1918	£2 10 0
	John Doeg	John Stephen	13.2.1919	£2 10 0
	Henry Doeg	Henry Hunter	13.2.1919	£2 10 0
	Robert Harrison	Robert Bell	27.12.1920	£2 10 0
	John George Boutland	Robert Pringle	26.12.1932	£2 10 0
	Alfred Hall Carter	Alfred	26.12.1933	£2 10 0
	Eric Carter	Alfred	26.12.1936	£2 10 0
	Eric Boutland	Robert Pringle	26.12.1945	£2 10 0
	John Anthony Boutland	John George	26.12.1949	£2 10 0
	Albe t Boutland	Robert Pringle	1.10.1954	£0 10 0

(C) Members of the Company by Presentation

Date	Name	Father's Christian Name	Occupation	Paid for Freedom
2.2.1738	William Carre		Mayor of Newcastle	
14.9.1773	Nathaniel Bayles		Barber Surgeon and Free Burgess	
14.9.1773	Henry Gibson		Barber Surgeon and Free Burgess	
14.9.1773	Alexander Adams		Hoastman and Free Burgess	
14.9.1773	Nicholas Tyzack		Barber Surgeon and Free Burgess	
14.9.1773	William Smith		Barber Surgeon and Free Burgess	
14.9.1773	Matthew Laidler		Baker and Brewer and Free Burgess	
14.9.1773	Benjamin Brunton		Cordwainer and Free Burgess	
14.9.1773	Thomas Maddison		Bricklayer and Free Burgess	
14.9.1773	William Addison		Barber Surgeon and Free Burgess	£10 0 0
5.3.1821[1]	Joseph Farrington	Richard	House Carpenter and Free Burgess	£11 17 6
27.12.1822[2]	William Smith	Thomas	Ropemaker and Free Burgess	£0 10 6
1.10.1954[2]	John William Porter			£0 10 6
1.10.1954	John Nicholson			£0 10 6
[?]1955	Albert Purcell Ions	Albert		£0 10 6
30.6.1955	William Henry Ions			
[?]1955	Leo Stanislaus Fenwick			
[?]1955	J. J. Taylor			
[?]1957	Robert Williau Miller	William Richard		£0 10 6
9.6.1958	Norman Harry Pescod			£0 10 6
9.6.1958	Eric Pescod			
[?]1958	John Joseph Fairs	Robert Roy		
22.6.1960	Ralph Thomas Fenwick	Leo Stanislous		

[1] [There is no evidence to show that these two were apprenticed as shipwrights, and the entry for their freedom specifically states that they were the sons of freemen of other companies rather than, as was normal, the apprentices of a particular shipwright. In the absence of other information they are therefore assumed to have been made members by presentation.]

[2] [From Porter onwards, with the re-organisation of the Company, I have treated all freedoms as being by presentation, since there is no direct patrimony link, except where sons of members made free by presentation after 1954 have themselves been made free and this familial relationship is not always clear from the records.]

Date	Name	Father's Christian Name	Occupation	Paid for Freedom
	Clifford Armstrong			
	John Thomas Armstrong			£0 10 6
	Kenneth Armstrong			£0 10 6
	David S. Fairs			
	Robert Roy Fairs			£0 10 6
	John William Gilchrist	John William		£0 10 6
	Ephraim Gilchrist	John William		
	Henry Gilchrist			
	Edward Hastings (formerly Hiscock)			£0 10 6
	J. W. Hiscock			
	Albert Ions			£0 10 6
	Raymond Ions			
	William Ions			
	William Roy Ions			£0 10 6
	William Richard Miller			
	Joseph Smart Nichols			
	Frederick Nicholson			
	John F. Pashley			£0 10 6
	Norman A. Pescod			
	William Renshaw			
	Derek Taylor	William Bell		
	Joseph Graham Taylor			
	J. W. B. Taylor	William Bell		
	Thomas Taylor			
	William Taylor			
	William Bell Taylor			
[25.6].1962	W. J. Taylor			£0 10 6
	Albert Hiscock			£0 10 6

296

Date	Name	Occupation	Father's Christian Name	Paid for Freedom
25.6.1962	Richard Ralph Hastings (formerly Hiscock)			£0 10 6
25.6.1962	Ian Frederick Miller		Alfred Peter	£0 10 6
25.6.1962	Harry Barras Taylor		Thomas Forster sen.	£0 10 6
25.6.1962	John Robert Taylor		Thomas Forster sen.	£0 10 6
25.6.1962	Thomas Forster Taylor jun.		Thomas Forster sen.	£0 10 6
25.6.1962	Thomas Forster Taylor sen.		William	£0 10 6
17.6.1963	Alfred Peter Miller			£0 10 6
17.6.1963	William Nichols			£0 10 6
17.6.1963	Alan Ions		William Henry	£0 10 6
17.6.1963	George Edward Ions			£0 10 6
17.6.1963	Stephen Graham Bell			£0 10 6
8.6.1964	John Richard Pescod			£0 10 6
8.6.1964	Thomas Petrie			£0 10 6
24.11.1964	James Miller			£0 10 6
12.7.1965	John William Gilchrist			£0 10 6
5.6.1967	Leonard Raymond Fenwick		Leo Stanislous	£0 10 6
17.6.1968				£0 10 6

APPENDIX II OFFICERS OF THE COMPANY

(A) STEWARDS

27 Dec.

1671[1]	Matthew Hutchinson,		Thomas Peacock
1672	John Watson		Thomas Steele
1673	Thos Steele		Thos Fenwicke
1674	—	do	—
1675	John Watson		Cuthbert Bone
1676	John Colier		Thomas Fenwicke
1677	Henry Cooke		John Watson
1678	Nicholas Dent		Thomas Fenwicke
1679	John Beckwith		—do—
1680	—	do	—
1681	Thomas Fenwicke		John Milbourne
1682	Thomas Poyde		Matthew Hutchinson
1683	—	do	—
1684	—do—		Thomas Wrangham
1685	—	do	—
1686	—	do	—
1687	Thos Fenwicke		John Colier
1688	—do—		Matthew Hutchinson
1689	Thomas Barber		Richard Coates
1690	Thos Fenwicke		—do—
1691	Thos Campling		—do—
1692	Thos Fenwicke		—do—
1693	Daniell Lawson		John Porter
1694	Thos Fenwicke		Richard Coates
1695	—	do	
1696	Wm Cooke		Wm Struther
1697	Thos Fenwicke		Mark Bell
1698	—	do	—
1699	Richard Coates		—do—
1700	Thomas Liddle		Thomas Wallas
1701	Jeremiah Cooke		Richard Coates
1702	Richard Coates		Wm Strother
1703	William Strother		Thomas Liddell
1704	—	do	—

[1] The stewards were elected on the Head Meeting day, 27th December, to serve for the ensuing year.

1705	George Taylor		Richard Urwen
1706	—	do	—
1707	—	do	—
1708	Richard Urwen		Thomas Forster
1709	Edward Potts		—do—
1710	Thomas Wallas		George Hymers
1711	George Taylor		Edward Potts
1712	Edward Potts		Richard Urwen
1713	Richard Urwin		Thomas Reed jun.
1714	—	do	—
1715	—	do	—
1716	John Beckwith		George Hindmarsh
1717	Richard Urwen		Thomas Reed jun.
1718	Richard Urwin		Thomas Wallas
1719	Thomas Wallas		John Snowball
1720	Richard Urwin		Thomas Wallas
1721	Wm Trewhitt		George Hindmarsh
1722	Thomas Wallas		Wm Trewhitt
1723	—	do	—
1724	—	do	—
1725	—	do	—
1726	Wm Trumble		Thomas Wallas
1727	Wm Trewhitt		Ralph Stell
1728	Thomas Wallas		Wm Trewhitt
1729	Wm Turnbull sen.		Cuthbert Preston
1730	Richard Wilson		Ralph Stell
1731	Wm Turnbull sen.		Wm Trewhitt
1732	—	do	—
1733	—do—		Richard Wilson
1734	Wm Trewhett		Cuthbert Preston
1735	—	do	—
1736	—	do	—
1737	Wm Turnbull		Thomas Taylor
1738	—	do	—
1739	Ralph Stell		Cuthbert Preston
1740	—do—		Thos Taylor
1741	Wm Park		Ralph Stell
1742	—do—		Thos Taylor
1743	—	do	—
1744	Ralph Stell		—do—
1745	—	do	—
1747	Wm Marshall		
1748	Thomas Taylor		Wm Marshall

1749	Ralph Stell		Wm Wilkinson jun.
1750	—	do	—
1751	Wm Wilkinson jun.		Roger Almory
1752	—	do	—
1753	—	do	—
1754	—	do	—
1755	Wm Wilkinson		Roger Almory
1756	—	do	
1757	Roger Almory		Francis Trewhitt
1758	Francis Trewhitt		Jacob Fisher
1759	—	do	—
1760	—do—		John Rennoldson
1761	Wm Wilkinson jun.		John Burrell jun.
1762	—do—		John Burrell
1763	—do—		Jacob Fisher
1764	Jacob Fisher		John Coxon
1765	—	do	—
1766	—do—		Lyonel Robson jun.
1767	—	do	—
1768	—	do	—
1769	Lyonel Robson jun.		John Spencer
1770	—	do	—
1771	—	do	—
1772	Lyonel Robson		Jacob Fisher
1773	Lyonel Robson jun.		—do—
1774	Jacob Fisher		Thomas Curry
1775	—	do	—
1776	—do—		Lionel Robson
1777	—	do	—
1778	—	do	—
1779	—	do	—
1780	—	do	—
1781	—	do	—
1782	—	do	—
1783	—	do	—
1784	—	do	—
1785	Thomas Curry		Lionel Robson
1786	—	do	—
1787	Lionel Robson		Thomas Curry
1788	—do—		George Cram
1789	—	do	—
1790	—	do	—
1791	—	do	—
1792	—	do	—

1793	Lionel Robson	do	George Cram
1794	—	do	—
1795	—	do	—
1796	—do—		Robert Gothard
1797	—	do	—
1798	—	do	—
1799	—	do	—
1800	—	do	—
1801	—	do	—
1802	—	do	—
1803	—do—		Henry Wright
1804	—	do	—
1805	Henry Wright		Alexander Doeg
1806	—	do	—
1807	Wm Laslie		—do—
1808	—	do	—
1809	—	do	—
1810	—	do	—
1811	—	do	—
1812	—	do	—
1813	—	do	—
1814	—do—		Wm Wright
1815	Robt Gothard		—do—
1816	—	do	—
1817	—	do	—
1818	—	do	—
1819	—	do	—
1820	—	do	—
1821	—	do	—
1822	—	do	—
1823	Wm Wright		Joseph Farrington
1824	Joseph Farrington		Wm Wright jun.
1825	Wm Wright jun.		Joseph Coxon
1826	—	do	—
1827	—	do	—
1828	—	do	—
1829	—	do	—
1830	Wm Wright		Thos Sadler
1831	—	do	—
1834	William Wright		Ambrose Hopper
1841	A. Hopper		C. Ker Spence

1847	Ambrose Hopper		John Doeg
1848	—do—		John Hall
1849	—	do	—
1850	—	do	—
1851	—	do	—
1854	Ambrose Hopper		John Doeg
1855	—	do	—
1856	—	do	—
1857	—	do	—
1858	—	do	—
1859	—	do	—
1860	—	do	—
1861	—	do	—
1862	—	do	—
1863	—	do	—
1864	—	do	—
1865	—	do	—
1866	—	do	—
1867	—	do	—
1868	—	do	—
1869	—	do	—
1870	Richard Hopper		John Hall
1872	Richard Hopper		John Hall
1873	—	do	—
1875	John Hall		John Morris
1876	—	do	—
1888	John Hall		John Morris
1889	—	do	—
1890	—	do	—
1891	—	do	—
1892	—	do	—
1893	John Doeg		—do—
1894	—	do	—
1895	—	do	—
1896	—	do	—
1897	—	do	—
1898	—	do	—
1899	—	do	—
1900	—	do	—
1901	—do—		Robt B. Harrison jun.

1902	John Doeg		Robt B. Harrison jun.
1903	—	do	—
1904	—	do	—
1905	John C. Boutland		—do—
1909	John C. Boutland		R. B. Harrison jun.
1919	John C. Boutland		H. Hunter Doeg
1920	—do—		R. B. Harrison
1921	—	do	—
1922	—	do	—
1923	—do—		R. P. Boutland
1924	—	do	—
1925	—	do	—
1926	—	do	—
1927	R. P. Boutland		Alfred Carter
1928	—	do	—
1929	—	do	—
1930	—	do	—
1931	—	do	—
1932	—	do	—
1933	—	do	—
1934	—	do	—
1935	R. P. Boutland		Alfred Carter
1936	—	do	—
1937	—	do	—
1938	—	do	—
1939	—	do	—
1945	R. P. Boutland		Alfred Carter
1946	—	do	—
1947	—	do	—
1948	—do—		John George Boutland
1949	—	do	—
1950	—do—		Eric Boutland
1951	—	do	—
1952	—	do	—
1 Oct.			
1954	Eric Boutland		J. W. Porter
30 June			
1955	—	do	—
18 June			
1956	—	do	—

27 Feb.
1957   J. W. Porter   J. Nicholson
9 June

1958	—	do	—
1959	—	do	—

20 June

1960	—	do	—
1961	—	do	—

25 June

1962	—	do	—

17 June

1963	—	do	—

8 June
1964   J. Nicholson   J. W. Porter
12 July

1965	—	do	—

13 June

1966	—	do	—

5 June
1967   —do—   Alfred P. Miller
17 June

1968	—	do	—

(B) *OVERSEERS*

27 Dec.

1712[2]	John Snawball sen.	Robt Richardson
1713	George Taylor	Ralph Hoxton
1714	John Taylor	Charles Emmerson
1715	George Taylor	Cuthbert Preston
1716	John Trewhitt	Henry Robinson
1717	Richard Wilson	Robt Coulson
1718	John Trewhitt	Henry Robinson
1719	Francis Watson	John Thowburn
1720	Wm Trumble sen.	Richard Wilson
1721	Ralph Stell	Robert Wallas
1722	Wm Rennison	John Thowburn
1723	Wm Trumble jun.	Ralph Stell
1724	Robt Simpson	Robt Wallas
1725	John Thowburn	Thomas Taylor
1726	Thomas Forster	George Maughlin

[2] The overseers were elected on the Head Meeting day, 27th December, to serve for the ensuing year.

1727	Ed. Trewhitt		Wm Stawart
1728	James Wallis		Thomas Harrison
1729	Andrew Hay		Charles Lucas
1730	John Thowburn		Wm Watson
1731	George Storey		Thomas Taylor
1732	Thomas Taylor		Wm Henderson
1733	John Semple		Andrew Haxton
1734	Thomas Taylor		Thomas Harrison
1735	Ralph Stell		John Coxon
1736	John Trewhitt		Robert Cay
1737	Andrew Haxton		Wm Watson
1738	—	do	—
1739	John Trewhitt		Robt Cay
1740	Andrew Haxton		Wm Watson
1741	John Trewhitt		Andrew Haxton
1742	Lyonel Robson		—do—
1743	John Coxon		Robt Cay
1744	John Trewhitt		—do—
1745	Lyonel Robson		Francis Trewhitt
1749	Paul Park		Francis Trewhitt
1750	Francis Trewhitt		Thos Taylor
1751	Thomas Taylor		Francis Trewhitt
1752	—	do	—
1753	Paul Park		Thomas Taylor
1754	Lyonell Robson		—do—
1755	Thomas Taylor		Paul Park
1756	Paul Park		Lyonel Robson
1757	—	do	—
1758	—	do	—
1759	Lyonel Robson sen.		Thomas Taylor sen.
1760	—	do	—
1761	—	do	—
1762	—	do	—
1763	—	do	—
1764	John Thackry		Thos Taylor jun.
1765	Lyonel Robson sen.		John Spencer
1766	—do—		John Almory
1767	John Spencer		Joseph Moore
1768	Lyonel Robson sen.		John Spencer
1769	—do—		Edward Laing
1770	—do—		John Almory
1771	—do—		John Thackry
1772	—do—		Michael McTosh

1773	Lyonel Robson sen.		Michael Mackintosh
1774	James White		Joseph Nixon
1775	Thomas Wilson		James White
1776	Thomas Taylor		—do—
1777	—	do	—
1778	James White		Michael Mackintosh
1779	—	do	—
1780	—	do	—
1781	Thomas Taylor		James White
1782	—do—		John Almory
1783	James White		Thomas Taylor
1784	—	do	—
1785	—	do	—
1786	—	do	—
1787	Jacob Fisher		—do—
1788	Thomas Taylor		Wm Charlton
1789	—	do	—
1790	—	do	—

1791 "The office of overseer was this day unanimously voted to be of no use and ordered to be abolished from this day."

(C) *THE TWELVE*
27 Dec.

1712 John Trewhitt, Thos Forster, Andrew Dawson, Richard Coates, George Taylor, Robt Walton, John Taylor, Thos Forster jun., John Beckwith jun., Thomas Wallas, James Lowson, George Hymers.

1713 Marmaduke Smithson, John Goodson, Thomas Campion, Edward Potts, Thos Wrangham, Robt Walton, John Taylor, Thos Forster jun., Charles Emmerson, Wm Fletcher, James Lowson, George Hymers.

1714 Rich'd Coates, John Goodson, Thomas Campion, George Taylor, Robt Hoxton, Robt Walton, Thos Wrangham, Wm Hanby, John Beckwith, Roger Durham jun., James Lowson, George Hindmarsh.

1715 Rich'd Coates, John Goodson, Thomas Campion, Edward Potts, Averah Trewhitt sen., Robt Walton, Thos Wrangham, Wm Hanby, John Beckwith, Wm Fletcher jun., James Lowson, John Taylor.

1716 John Trewhitt, John Goodson, Jeremiah Cook, Edward Potts, Averah Trewhitt sen., Richard Urwen sen., Thos Reed jun., Robt Richardson, Averah Trewhitt jun., Wm Fletcher James Lowson, Cuthbert Preston.

1717 M. Smithson, John Goodson, Thomas Campion, Edward Potts, Averah Trewhitt sen., Richard Coates, Wm Reed, Robt Walton, Thos Wrangham, John Beckwith, Thos Wallas, Roger Durham jun.

1718 Jeremiah Cooke, John Goodson, Thomas Campion, Edward Potts, George Taylor, John Taylor, Geo. Hindmarsh, Cuthbert Preston, James Lowson, John Beckwith, James Wallas, Roger Durham jun.

1719 Thos Campion, George Taylor, Edw'd Potts, John Taylor, Wm Trewhitt, James Lowson, James Wallas, Roger Durham jun., Geo. Hindmarsh, Henry Robinson, Bryan Wall, Cuthbert Preston.

1720 John Reed, George Taylor, Wm Reed, John Taylor, Averah Trewhitt, James Lowson, Thos Wrangham, Wm Trewhitt, Geo. Hindmarsh, John Snowball, Bryan Wall, Cuthbert Preston.

1721 Thomas Wallas, George Taylor, Edw'd Potts, Richard Urwen sen., Averah Trewhitt, John Wallas, John Taylor sen., Wm Trumble jun., John Charleton sen., Robt. Coulson, Joseph Campion, Cuthbert Preston.

1722 Richard Wilson sen., George Taylor, Edw'd Potts, Ralph Stell, Averah Trewhitt, Thomas Wilson, John Taylor sen., Wm Trumble jun., George Gordon, Robt Wallas, Joseph Campion, Cuthbert Preston.

1723 Jeremiah Cook, George Taylor, George Storey, Richard Wilson, Averah Trewhitt, Thomas Wilson, John Taylor sen., Robt. Coulson, John Reed, Robt Wallas, Joseph Campion, Edw'd Trewhitt.

1724 Jeremiah Cook, John Wallas, George Storey, Wm Trumble jun., Wm Trumble sen., Willoughby Hall, John Taylor sen., Robt Coulson, Thos Forster, Ralph Stell, Joseph Campion, Edw'd Trewhitt.

1725 Jeremiah Cook, John Wallas, Thos Wrangham, Roger Durham, Geo. Hindmarsh, Cuthbert Preston, John Taylor sen., John Taylor jun., John Reed, John Lattiney, Joseph Campion, Edw'd Trewhitt.

1726 John Thowburn, Thomas Taylor, Robt Coulson, George Storey, Ralph Stell, Cuthbert Preston, Wm Trumble jun., Jeremiah Simpson, Wm Trewhitt, John Lattiney, Joseph Campion, John Trumble.

1727 Wm Turnbull sen., Thomas Wallas sen., Geo. Hindmarsh, Wm Turnbull jun., Robt Coulson, Cuthbert Preston, John Thowburn, Wm Barber, John Lettiney, Wm Thompson, Robt Wallis, Thos Marlay.

1728   John Taylor, Robt Simpson, Wm Turnbull sen., Wm Turnbull jun., Robt Coulson, Cuthbert Preston, Ralph Stell, Thomas Taylor, John Lettiney, John Coxon, Edward Trewhitt, Robt Wallis.

1729   Thomas Forster sen., Robt Simpson, Thomas Wallis, Wm Turnbull jun., Robt Coulson, Wm Trewhitt, Ralph Stell, Thomas Taylor, Thos Wilson, John Thowburn, Thos Harrison, Wm Watson.

1730   Wm Turnbull sen., Wm Rennison, Wm Park, John Lee, Wm Staward, Cuthbert Preston, Andrew Hay, John Coxon, Thos Wilson, Charles Lucas, Thos Harrison, Ralph Ord.

1731   Thos Forster sen., Richard Wilson, Wm Park, Wm Turnbull jun., Ralph Stell, Robt Coulson, John Turnbull, Wm Barber, Edw'd Trewhitt, John Lettiney, Robt Wallis jun., Thos Forster jun.

1732   Robt Simpson, Richard Wilson, Wm Park, Wm Turnbull jun., Ralph Stell, John Taylor, John Turnbull, Wm Barber, Edw'd Trewhitt, John Lettiney, Robt Wallis jun., George Storey.

1733   Robt Simpson, Wm Bolam, John James, Andrew Hay, Abraham Dowson, John Taylor, Henry Ovington, Thomas Harrison, George Mauris, Wm Watson, John Lee, Thos Forster jun.

1734   Wm Turnbull sen., George Storey, Wm Park, Wm Rennison, Ralph Stell, Wm Turnbull jun., Robt Coulson, John Taylor, John Coxon, Edw'd Trewhitt, Wm Watson, Thos Wallis jun.

1735   Wm Turnbull, George Storey, Wm Rennison, Robt Coulson, John Taylor, John James, John Turnbull, Andrew Hay, Thos Harrison, Edw'd Trewhitt, Wm Watson, Thos Wallis jun.

1736   Ralph Stell, George Storey, Bryan Wall, Robt Coulson, Thomas Taylor, John Turnbull, Andrew Hay, John Coxon, Edw'd Trewhitt, Robt Young, John Burrell, Ralph Ord.

1737   Thos Wrangham, Thos Forster, John Taylor, John James, John Thowburn, Robt Briggs, Thos Harrison, Ralph Lowson, Ralph Reed, Lyonel Robson, Thos Wallis jun., Thos Forster jun.

1738   Thos Wrangham, Thos Forster, Wm Park, John Taylor, John James, John Thowburn, Wm Henderson, Thos Harrison, Ralph Lowson, John Lee, Thos Wallis jun., Thos Forster jun.

1739   Wm Park, Jeremiah Milburn, Robt Coulson, Wm Staward, John Turnbull, John Carrier, John Coxon, Ed. Trewhitt, Ralph Reed, Andrew Haxton, Wm Watson, John Burrell.

1740   Bryan Wall, Robt Coulson, Wm Staward, Cuthbert Preston,

John Taylor, John Turnbull, Wm Henderson, John Coxon, Thos Harrison, Ralph Reed, Lyonell Robson, Thomas Wallis.

1741 Rich'd Wilson, Jeremiah Milburn, Robt Coulson, Cuthbert Preston, John Taylor, Thos Taylor, John Turnbull, Andrew Hay, John Carrier, Wm Watson, John Burrell, Thomas Wallis.

1742 Rich'd Wilson, Ralph Stell, Robt Coulson, John Taylor, John Thowburn, Abraham Dowson, Andrew Hay, John Carrier, Ralph Lowson, Thos Wallis, James Eyons, Francis Trewhitt.

1743 Rich'd Wilson, Ralph Stell, John Taylor, John James, John Thowburn, Wm Henderson, Andrew Hay, John Carrier, Ralph Lowson, Andrew Haxton, Wm Watson, Francis Trewhitt.

1744 Wm Park, Rich'd Wilson, Cuthbert Preston, John Taylor, John Turnbull, John Thowburn, Wm Henderson, Andrew Hay, John Carrier, Ralph Lowson, Andrew Haxton, Wm Watson.

1745 Wm Park, Rich'd Wilson, Cuthbert Preston, John Taylor, John Thowburn, John Turnbull, James White, John Carrier, John Burrell, John Fawdon, Wm Wilkinson jun., Enoch White.

1749 Wm Park, Wm Bolam, John Taylor, Thos Taylor sen., John Turnbull, Lionell Robson, John Burrell, Wm Marshall, Robert Goddart, James White jun., Robt Wilson, Roger Almory.

1750 Wm Park, John Taylor, John Turnbull, Lyonell Robson, John Burrell, Wm Marshall, Robt Goddart, John Thackwray, Paul Park, John Goddart, Robt Wilson, Roger Almory.

1751 Ralph Stell, John Turnbull, Lyonel Robson, John Goddart, John Thackwray, Paul Park, James White jun., Robt Wilson, Robert French, Stephen Goddart, John Coxon, John Almory.

1752 Ralph Stell, Bryan Wall, John Turnbull, Lyonell Robson, John Burrell, Michael Tosh, Robert Gothart, Paull Park, John Gothart, James White jun., Robt French, Bryan Wall jun.

1753 Bryan Wall, John Carrier, Ralph Lowson, Lyonell Robson, William Watson, John Fawdon, Will'm Charlton, John Gothart, Francis Trewhitt, John Rennison, Jacob Fisher, John Coxon.

1754   John Turnbull, John Carrier, Edward Trewhit, Ralph Lowson, Wm Charlton, Robt Gothart, John Gothart, Francis Trewhitt, John Headlam, John Rennison, Jacob Fisher, John Coxon.

1755   John Rennison, John Coxon, John Carrier, Wm Charlton, Jacob Fisher, John Trumble, John Fawdon, Francis Trewhitt, John Gothard, William Henderson, George Rennison, Robt Gothard.

1756   John Rennison, Jacob Fisher, George Cram, Wm Henderson, Francis Trewhitt, John Turnbull, John Taylor jun., George Rennison, John Coxon, John Carrier, John Gothard, Edward Durham.

1757   John Carrier, Edward Durham, William Wilkinson, John Thackwray, John Gothard, George Rennison, Thomas Wilson, Jacob Fisher, John Coxon, George Cram, William Henderson, John Ridley.

1758   John Carrier, Edward Durham, James Eyons, John Thackwray, Thomas Wilson, John Gothard, Robert French, Roger Almory, Robert Thompson, John Coxon, John Almory, John Semple jun.

1759   John Carrier, Edward Durham, Thomas Wilson, John Gothard, James White, Robert French, George Rennison, John Park, John Coxon, George Cram, Thos Taylor jun., John Spencer.

1760   Jacob Fisher, John Thackwray, Thomas Wilson, Robt French, John Coxon, Geo. Rennoldson, Joseph Moor, John Spencer, Thos Taylor jun., Wm Carse, John Brydon, Roger Almory.

1761   Jacob Fisher, Joseph Moor, Thos Taylor jun., John Spencer, Geo. Cram, Thos Curry, Thos Wilson, Wm Carse, John Thackwray, John Johnson, Robt French, Bartholomew Barker.

1762   John Thackwray, Thos Wilson, Jacob Fisher, John Coxon, Wm Carse, Joseph Moore, Thos Curry, Wm Thobourn, Thos Taylor jun., John Spencer, Robt Wilson, John Johnson.

1763   John Thackry, Thos Wilson, John Coxon, Wm Carse, Wm Ostens, Wm Thobourn, Jos. Moore, Thos Taylor jun., Lionel Robson jun., John Johnson, John Spencer, Robt Wilson.

1764   Wm Charlton, Thos Wilson, Thos Taylor sen., John Rennoldson, James White, Geo. Rennoldson, Thos Curry, Geo. Maughline, Joseph Moore, Lionel Moore, Lionel Robson jun., John Spencer.

1765   Wm Charlton, Thos Wilson, Thos Taylor sen., John Rennoldson, James White, Ephraim Curry, Thos. Curry, Wm

Ramsay, Joseph Moore, Thos Taylor jun., Lionel Robson jun., Robt Wilson.

1766   Wm Charlton, John Thackry, Thos Wilson, Thos Taylor sen., James White, Ephraim Curry, Geo. Maughlin, Joseph Moore, Thos Taylor jun., T. E. Headlam, John Spencer, Robt Wilson.

1767   Wm Charlton, John Thackry, Thos Wilson, Thos Taylor sen., Edward Laing, James White, John Almory, Wm Carse, Thos Curry, Thos Taylor jun., T. E. Headlam, Robt Wilson.

1768   Wm Charlton, Thos Wilson, John Thackry, Thos Taylor, James White, Wm Carse, John Almory, Thos Curry, T. E. Headlam, Thos Taylor jun., Robt Wilson, John Eyons.

1769   Wm Charlton, Thos Taylor sen., John Thackry, James White, Wm Wilkinson, John Almory, Thos Curry, Thos Taylor jun., T. E. Headlam, Robt Wilson, John Eyons, Robt Rankin.

1770   Wm Charlton, Wm Wilkinson, Thos Wilson, Thos Taylor sen., Ed. Laing, Jacob Fisher, Thos Curry, Thos Taylor jun., T. E. Headlam, Robt Wilson, Wm Cook, Robt Rankin.

1771   Wm Charlton, Thos Wilson, Thos Taylor sen., James White, Jacob Fisher, Wm Carse, John Almory, Thos Curry, T. E. Headlam, Robt Wilson, Wm Cook, Robt Rankin.

1772   Wm Charlton, Thos Wilson, Thos Taylor sen., James White, John Almory, Wm Carse, Thos Curry, T. E. Headlam, John Spencer, Wm Cook, Robt Rankin, Joseph Nixon.

1773   Thos Wilson, Thos Taylor sen., John Rennoldson, James White, John Almory, Wm Carse, Thos Curry, T. E. Headlam, John Spencer, Wm Cook, Robt Rankin, Joseph Nixon.

1774   Lionel Robson sen., Thos Wilson, Thos Taylor, Edward Laing, John Rennoldson, John Almory, Wm Carse, Lionel Robson jun., T. E. Headlam, John Eyons, Robt Rankin, Matthew Pringle.

	1st four	2nd four	3rd four
1780	John Rennoldson	Thos Curry	Matthew Pringle
	Wm Carse	Wm Laslie	Thos Wilson
	T. E. Headlam	John Almory	Edward Laing
	Wm Charlton	Joseph Nixon	Robert McIntosh
	1st four	2nd four	3rd four
1781	T. E. Headlam	Wm Lambert	Thos Wilson
	Thos Curry	Joseph Nixon	John Almory
	Wm Laslie	John Bell	Matthew Pringle
	Wm Carse	Wm Charlton	John Rennoldson

	1st four	2nd four	3rd four
1782	Thos Curry	Wm Lambert	Wm Laslie
	T. E. Hedlam	Charles Steward	Wm Carse
	Thos Wilson	Wm Charlton	Geo. Reay
	Joseph Nixon	John Reynoldson	John Bell
	1st four	2nd four	3rd four
1783	Thos Curry	Wm Carse	John Rennoldson
	T. E. Headlam	Wm Lambert	Wm Laslie
	Thos Wilson	Charles Stewart	John Bell
	Joseph Nixon	Wm Charlton	Thos Guthery
	1st four	2nd four	3rd four
1784	Thos Curry	John Bell	John Rennoldson
	T. E. Headlam	Wm Laslie	Thos Guthery
	Thos Wilson	Joseph Nixon	Wm Lambert
	Wm Carse	Wm Charlton	George Wray
	1st four	2nd four	3rd four
1785	T. E. Headlam	Charles Stewart	Wm Charlton
	John Rennoldson	David Rennoldson	Jacob Fisher
	Wm Carse	Wm Lambert	Wm Laslie
	John Bell	Henry Wright	John Almory
	1st four	2nd four	3rd four
1786	T. E. Headlam	Charles Stuart	John Bell
	John Rennoldson	David Rennoldson	Henry Wright
	Wm Laslie	Wm Carse	Alexander Doag
	George Cram	Wm Curry	Matthew Henderson
	1st four	2nd four	3rd four
1787	Wm Lambert	Charles Stuart	John Bell
	T. E. Headlam	Wm Carse	Joseph Nixon
	George Cram	Robert Gothard	Matthew Henderson
	John Rennoldson	Wm Curry	Wm Charlton
	1st four	2nd four	3rd four
1788	T. E. Headlam	Wm Laslie	Robert Gothard
	Wm Carse	Joseph Nixon	Ephraim Curry
	Charles Stuart	Wm Curry	John Almory
	Matthew Henderson	Wm Lambert	Thomas Pattison
	1st four	2nd four	3rd four
1789	T. E. Headlam	Joseph Nixon	Matthew Henderson
	Wm Carse	Thomas Pattison	John Almory
	Wm Laslie	Robert Gothard	Alexander Doag
	Wm Lambert	Ephraim Curry	Thos Guthrie
	1st four	2nd four	3rd four
1790	T. E. Headlam	Thos Pattison	Alexander Doag
	Wm Carse	Matthew Henderson	John Almory

	1st four	2nd four	3rd four
	Wm Laslie	Ephraim Curry	Thos Guthrie
	Wm Lambert	Robert Gothard	Joseph Nixon
1791	as for 1790		
1792	as for 1790		
1793	T. E. Headlam	Robt Gothard	Alexander Doag
	Wm Carse	Ephraim Curry	John Almory
	Wm Laslie	Matthew Henderson	Thos Guthrie
	Wm Lambert	Thomas Pattison	Joseph Nixon
1794	T. E. Headlam	Robt Gothard	John Almory
	Wm Laslie	Matthew Henderson	Thomas Guthrie
	Wm Lambert	Thomas Pattison	Joseph Nixon
	Ephraim Curry	Alexander Doag	John Macleod
1795	T. E. Headlam	Robt Gothard	John Almory
	Wm Laslie	Matthew Henderson	Thomas Guthrie
	Wm Lambert	Alexander Doag	Joseph Nixon
	Ephraim Curry	Henry Charlton	Robt McIntosh
1796	T. E. Headlam	Ephraim Curry	John Almory
	George Cram	Matthew Henderson	Thomas Guthrie
	Wm Lambert	Alexander Doag	Joseph Nixon
	Wm Laslie	Henry Charlton	Robert Macintosh
1797	as for 1796		
1798	as for 1796		
1799	as for 1796		
1800	T. E. Headlam	Matthew Henderson	John Almory
	George Cram	Alexander Doag	Thomas Guthrie
	Wm Lambert	Henry Charlton	John McLeod
	Wm Laslie	Henry Wright	Joseph Nixon
1801	T. E. Headlam	Matthew Henderson	John Almory
	Wm Lambert	Alexander Doeg	Thomas Guthrie
	Wm Laslie	Henry Charlton	George Young
	Wm Carse	Henry Wright	John McLeod
1802	as for 1801		

	1st four	2nd four	3rd four
1803	T. E. Headlam	Matthew Hender-son	George Cram
	Wm Lambert	Robt Gothard	John McLeod
	Wm Laslie	Wm Carse	George Young
	Alex. Doeg	H'y Charlton	John Turner
	1st four	2nd four	3rd four
1804	T. E. Headlam	Matthew Hender-son	George Cram
	Wm Lambert	Robt Gothard	John McLeod
	Wm Laslie	Wm Carse	John Bell
	Alex. Doeg	H'y Charlton	John Turner
	1st four	2nd four	3rd four
1805	T. E. Headlam	Matthew Hender-son	George Cram
	Thos Duncan	Robt Gothard	John McLeod
	Wm Laslie	Wm Carse	John Bell
	James Carse	H'y Charlton	John Turner
1806	as for 1805		
	1st four	2nd four	3rd four
1807	John Bell	H'y Charlton	Jos. Coxon
	Matt. Henderson	Wm Carse	Wm Wright
	Robt Gothard	Jos. Brown	T. E. Headlam
	John McLeod	James Carse	George Cram
1808	as for 1807		
	1st four	2nd four	3rd four
1809	H'y Wright	H'y Charlton	Jos. Coxon
	Matt. Henderson	Wm Carse	Wm Wright
	Robt Gothard	Jos. Brown	Simon Temple
	John McLeod	James Carse	Wm Smith
1810	as for 1809		
	1st two	2nd two	3rd two
1813	Robt Gothard	Wm Carse	John McLeod
	Wm Wright	Joseph Coxon	Matt. Henderson
	1st two	2nd two	3rd two
1814	Alex. Doeg	Wm Carss	Ephraim Henderson
	H'y Wright	Jos. Coxon	John McLeod
	1st two	2nd two	3rd two
1815	Wm Laslie	Alex. Doeg	Wm Carse
	Henry Wright	Joseph Coxon	James Evans
	1st two	2nd two	
1816	Wm Laslie	John McLeod	
	Thomas Sadler	John Gibson	

	1st two	2nd two	
1817	Wm Laslie	Jos. Coxon	
	Thomas Forsyth	Thomas Sadler	

	1st two	2nd two	3rd two
1818	Wm Laslie	Thomas Sadler	Wm Wilson
	Thomas Forsyth	John Gibson	Robt Smith
	4th two	5th two	6th two
	Alex. Doeg	John McLeod	Thomas Young
	H'y Wright	T. E. Headlam	Joseph Coxon

	1st two	2nd two	
1819	Jos. Coxon	Thomas Sadler	Wm Wilson
	John Gibson	Thomas Forsyth	

	1st two	2nd two	3rd two
1820	Wm Laslie	Thos Young	Jos. Coxon
	Thomas Sadler	Thos Forsyth	Wm Wilson
1821	As for 1820		

	1st two	2nd two	3rd two
1822	Wm Laslie	Wm Wilson	Alex. Doeg
	Thos Young	Jos. Farrington	Wm Wilson jun.

	1st two	2nd two	
1823	Wm Wilson	Thos Forsyth	Wm Wilson jun.
	Thos Sadler	Robt Gothard	

	1st two	2nd two	
1825	Wm Wright sen.	Wm Wilson	
	John Sadler	Wm Wilson jun.	

(4) *REPRESENTATIVES CHOSEN TO ELECT THE MAYOR OF NEWCASTLE*

27 Dec.

1715	Thos Reed jun.	1729	Thomas Wallas
1716	John Beckwith	1730	—do—
1717	—do—	1731	—do—
1718	Richard Urwin	1732	Wm Trewhitt
		1733	Thomas Wallis
1720	Thomas Wallas	1734	Wm Trewhitt
1721	—do—		
		1736	Wm Trewhitt
1724	Wm Trewhitt	1737	—do—
1725	—do—	1738	—do—
1726	Thomas Wallas		
1727	—do—	1742	Wm Park
1728	—do—		

1755	Roger Almory	1793	Lionel Robson
1756	Wm Wilkinson	1794	—do—
1757	Francis Trewhitt	1795	—do—
1758	—do—	1796	—do—
1759	—do—	1797	—do—
1760	Lyonel Robson jun.	1798	—do—
1761	Roger Almory	1799	—do—
1762	Francis Trewhitt	1800	—do—
1763	Wm Wilkinson jun.	1801	Wm Laslie
1764	Robert Wilson	1802	Lionel Robson
1765	John Coxon	1803	—do—
1766	Wm Wilkinson		
1767	Joseph Moore	1805	Alexander Doag
1768	John Spencer	1806	Wm Laslie
1769	T. E. Headlam	1807	—do—
1770	Lyonel Robson Jun.	1808	Alexander Doeg
1771	Robt Rankin	1809	—do—
1772	Lionel Robson jun.	1810	Wm Laslie
1773	T. E. Headlam		
1774	Lionel Robson jun.	1813	Wm Laslie
1776	Lionel Robson jun.	1815	Wm Laslie
1777	Lionel Robson	1816	—do—
1778	—do—	1817	—do—
1779	—do—	1818	Robert Gothard
1780	—do—	1819	—do—
1781	—do—	1820	Wm Wright
1782	Thomas Curry	1821	—do—
1783	Lionel Robson	1822	—do—
1784	—do—	1823	—do—
1785	—do—	1824	Joseph Farrington
1786	—do—	1825	Wm Wright jun.
1787	—do—	1826	—do—
1788	—do—	1827	—do—
1789	T. E. Headlam	1828	—do—
1790	Lionel Robson		
1791	—do—	1834	Ambrose Hopper
1792	—do—		

APPENDIX III—FINES

Fines levied on members for the year 1717
6 *Jan.* Meeting of the Stewards and Twelve   Thomas Reed, (absent)
7   Meeting of the Stewards and Twelve   Thomas Reed, James Lowson, Wm Fletcher
9   Meeting of the Stewards and Twelve   Thos Reed, Wm Fletcher
11 *March*   Meeting of the Stewards and Twelve   Wm Fletcher, Jeremiah Cooke
23 *April*   (Quarter Day) Meeting of the Whole Company

Absent [fine 6d]
Thomas Hudson, Thomas Campion, Wm Reed, Wm Wilkinson, Edward Blunt, Ed. Wilkinson, Ed. Slater, James Wilson, James Lowson, Roger Durham jun., Robt Collingwood, Arthur Liddle, Benjamin Gibson, John Ingledue, Geo. Kitchen, Wm Wilkinson, Ralph Stell, Joseph Haitor, Wm Fletcher jun., John Heeman, Thos Potts, John Thowburn, Robt Guy, John Reed,

Fines [6d each]	*30th January*
Working on New Years Day	Wm Parke & servant
Joseph Errington	Jeremiah Milburn & servant
Joseph Hayton	Geo. Farmer
	Roger Durham jun. & 2 men
St Paul's Day	John Snowball
John Snowball	Richard Trewhit
John Park	Robt Kirkeley
James Lowson	Arthur Lidle
Thos Wilson	Joseph Haytor
Geo. Wilson	
Roger Durham jun. & 2 men	
Richard Trewhit	*Candlemas Day*
Wm Trewhit	Wm Park & 1 man
Geo. Storey	Robt Akenside
Wm Hoxton	Roger Durham jun. & 3 men
Thos Laburn	Matthew Graham
Averah Trewhit jun.	Richard Wallas & 2 men
Ralph Reed jun.	Wm Bolam
Richard Wallas & 2 men	Ralph Reed jun.
Sam. Tulip	Averah Trewhit jun.
Paul Holliday & 1 man	Thomas Laburn

Arthur Lidle
Wm Wilson sen.
Wm Wilkinson jun.
Roger Jobling
Robt Kirkeley
Joseph Haytor

Easter Monday
James Fletcher
Bryan Wall

Overseers Presentments
Thomas Wallas work at a butt
wrought on a timber only a
strake [sic] betwixt them on
the starbard [sic] side forward
at the old pink upon the dock
insufficient.
George Farmer for an anchor
stock with a wedge put in on
board of an old goddart pink.
George Farmer for threatning
the two overseers to beat them.

24 June   (Quarter day)   Meeting of the whole Company

Absent
Nicholas Rain, Thomas Hudson, Jeremiah Cooke, Wm Wilkinson, Edward Blunt, Robt Pearson, John Fowler, Peter Farmer, Edward Wilkinson, Edward Slater, John Bootiman, John Wilkinson, Arthur Liddle, Benjamin Gibson, John Ingledue, Geo. Kitchen, Wm Wilkinson jun., Thos Shaftoe, Wm Fletcher jun., Wm Unthank, Wm Glenn, Matthew Graham, John Reed.

Henry Fletcher for refusing to pay 1/- fine for leaving his seat [in the meeting house]	3s 4d
John Shinon —do—	3s 4d
Henry Fletcher for refuseing to come to the Twelve when called on	3s 4d
Joseph Barber for going out of the meeting house without leave and saying that he would stay no longer	

St Mark's Day
James Wilson
Wm Trumble sen.
Samuel Tulipp
Wm Hoxton
Matthew Graham

29th May
James Wilson
John Hewitson
Henry Fletcher
Roger Jobling

Robt Kirkley
Wm Fletcher & 3 men

May Day
Wm Wilkinson jun.
Giles Gallon
James Wilson
Henry Fletcher
Robt Kirkley
John Hewitson
Matthew Graham
Robt Akenside

Ascension Day
Wm Fletcher & 3 men
Mary Wilkinsons son
James Wilson
John Hewitson
Bryan Wall

Whitson Monday
John Wilkinson sen.
Mary Wilkinson's son
Edw'd Wilkinson & 1 man
Thos Bell
Thos Potts
Wm Trumble sen.

Whitson Tuesday
Wm Fletcher & 3 men
Edw'd Wilkinson & 1 man
Mark Coxon
Richard Trewhitt

Wm Fletcher's work a plank wrought short at the hudden ends aft insufficient a butt wrought within seven inches of the skarf on the keel insufficient. His servant cawking of new work insufficient

30 Sept. (Quarter day) Meeting of the whole Company

Absent
Marmaduke Smithson, Wm Wilkinson sen., Thos Turner, Edw'd Wilkinson, James Wilkinson, Thomas Wallas, Robt Richardson, James Lowson, Robt Thackwray, Benjamin Gibson, John Ingledue, John Wilkinson, Wm Fletcher jun., Thos Pattison, Wm Unthank, John Thowburn, John Reed.

St Peter's Day
Wm Robinson
Thos Potts
John Wilkinson jun.
Wm Trumble jun.
Robt Thackwray
Robt Kirkley
Robt. Richardson & 1 man
John Harrison
Peter Lambert
Ralph Stell
Thomas Reed sen. & 2 Men
Richard Wallas & 2 men
Geo. Storey
Cuthbert Watson
Wm Wilson sen.
John James
Geo. Wilson
Thos Dixon

John Grey
Edw'd Wilkinson & 2 men
Henry Fletcher
Cuthbert Hall
Thos Laburn
Arthur Liddle
Thos Shaftoe (& for
    refuseing to pay—3s 4d)

St James's Day
Wm Wilson sen.
Giles Gallon
John Snowball
Thos Potts
Wm Trumble jun.
Robt Thackwray
John Wilkinson jun.
Rich'd Younghusband & 1 man
Wm Fletcher & 3 men

1st August
Wm Wilson sen.
Robt Thackwray
John Wilkinson jun.
Rich'd Younghusband's man
Ralph Bolam
John Trewhitt sen.
Thos Potts
Wm Trumble jun.
Mary Wilkinson's son

St Matthew's Day
Wm Fletcher & 1 man

Absent at Francis Burdon's
funeral

Henry Purvis
Cuthbert Watson
Thos Pattison
Thos Taylor
Absent at Edward Pott's wifes
funerall
Henry Fletcher
Wm Unthank
Thos Wrangham &
for refuseing to
pay   3s 4d
John Thowburn
Thos Potts
Peter Forseter for cawk-
ing at Mr Beckwiths
work insufficient   3s 4d

20 Dec. Meeting of the Stewards and Twelve
Thos Reed jun. for unbrotherly words to James Lowson
Geo. Hindmarsh for saying to John Beckwith Damn You
21 Meeting of the whole Company
Absent
Jeremiah Cooke, Wm Robinson, Cuthbert Preston, Geo. Gordon,
Jos. Campion, Geo. Collinson.
27 (Head Meeting Day)   Meeting of the whole Company
Absent
Thos Hudson, Jeremiah Cooke, Edw'd Potts, Robt Pearson,
Edw'd Wilkinson, James Wilkinson, Henry Cay, Robt Thack-
wray, Robt Collingwood, Francis Watson, Wm Renison, Ben-
jamin Gibson, John Ingledue, Wm Wilkinson jun., Joseph Barber,
Thomas Shaftoe, Joseph Haytor, Willoughby Hall, Wm Fletcher
jun., Wm Unthank, Mark Coxon, Thos Dixon, Geo. Gordon,
Robt Braidley.

Working on Holy Daies
St Luke Day
John Snowball

St Simon & St Jude
Mary Wilkinson's son
Henry Stainsby
Edward Wilkinson & 1 man
George Farrar

5 Nov. Gunpowder Treason
Edw'd Wilkinson & 1 man
Mary Wilkinson's son

Fines levied on members for the year 1768

Absences

5 April

John Trewhitt, John Fawdon, Rich. Shaw, Wm Rennoldson, John
Thackry, Fra. Trewhitt, John Wilson, John Gibson, Geo. Liddle,
Geo. Rennoldson, Robt Thompson, Ra. Hall, E. Curry, Jos.
Taylor, Geo. Smith, John Ellison, Wm Pearson, Geo. Cram, Ed.
Wilkinson, Wm Ostens, Chr. Henzell, Wm Ramshaw, Thos Allan,
Wm Donkin, Chas Watson, John Letteney, Cuth. Graham, John
Bridon, Wm Cook, Rich. Scott.

24 June

John Fawdon, Wm Marshall, Pere. Hutton, Thos Baird, Thos
Galley, Ed. Laing, John Wilson, Jas White, Rich. Shaw, John
Gibson, Wm Hindmarsh, Geo. Liddle, Geo. Rennoldson, Robt
Thompson, E. Curry, Jos. Taylor, B. Barker, Geo. Smith, John
Ellison, Wm Pearson, Geo. Cram, Ed. Wilkinson, Wm Ostens,
Chr. Henzell, Thos Allan, Wm Thobourn, John Spencer, Wm
Donkin, Hen. Doeg, Chas Watson, John Letteney, Cuth. Graham,
John Bridon, Wm Cook, Rich. Scott.

29 September

Geo. Collinson, Robt Wallis, John Fawdon, Wm Rennoldson,
M. McTosh, John Thackry, Thos Baird, Thos Galley, Thos
Taylor sen., Ed. Laing, Fra. Trewhitt, John Wilson, John Rennold-
son, Jas White, Rich. Shaw, John Gibson, Geo. Liddell, Geo.
Rennoldson, Robt Thompson, Ra. Hall, E. Curry, Jos. Taylor,
Geo. Smith, John Ellison, Wm Pearson, Geo. Cram, Ed. Wilkin-
son, Chr. Henzell, Wm Ramshaw, Thos Allan, Wm Thobourn,
Geo. Maughlin, Jos. Moor, Thos Taylor jun., Wm Donkin, Hen.
Doeg, Chas Watson, John Letteney, Cuth. Graham, John Bridon,
Wm Cook, Rich. Scott.

27 December

Geo. Collinson, Robt Wallis, John Fawdon, Wm Rennoldson, Pere. Hutton, Thos Baird, Thos Galley, Ed. Laing, John Wilson, John Rennoldson, Rich. Shaw, Geo. Liddell, Robt Thompson, E. Curry, Jos. Taylor, Geo. Smith, John Ellison, Ed. Wilkinson, Chr. Henzell, Wm Ramshaw, Thos Allan, Wm Thobourn, Jos. Moore, T. E. Headlam, Wm Donkin, Hen. Doeg, John Letteney, Wm Cook.

Quarterly Payments

January-March

John Trewhitt, Robt Wallis, Robt Briggs, John Fawdon, Joseph Edgar, Wm Rennoldson, Michael Mackintosh & son, John Thackry, Francis Trewhitt & 3 servants, John Rennoldson & 3 servants, Richard Shaw, John Gibson, Geo. Liddle, Geo. Rennoldson, Robt Thompson, Ralph Hall & 2 sons, E. Curry, Joseph Taylor, B. Barker, Geo. Smith & 3 servants, John Semple, John Ellison, Wm Pearson, Geo. Cram, Wm Ostens, Chr. Henzell, Wm Ramshaw, Thos Allan, Wm Thobourn, Geo. Maughlin, Wm Donkin, Henry Doeg, Charles Watson, John Letteney, Cuth. Graham, John Bridon, Wm Cook, Richard Scott.

April-June

John Trewhitt, Geo. Collinson, Robt Wallis, Robt Briggs, John Fawdon, Joseph Edgar, Wm Rennoldson, Peregrine Hutton, Wm Wilkinson, Michael McTosh, John Thackery, Thos Baird, Thos Galley, Ed. Laing, Francis Trewhitt & 3 servants, John Wilson, John Rennoldson & 3 servants, James White, Richard Shaw, John Gibson, Wm Hindmarsh, Geo. Liddle, Geo. Rennoldson, Robt Thompson, E. Curry, Joseph Taylor, B. Barker, Geo. Smith & 3 servants, John Semple, John Ellison, Wm Pearson, Geo. Cram, Ed. Wilkinson, Wm Ostens, Chr. Henzell, Thos Allan, Wm Thobourn, Geo. Maughlin, John Spencer & 2 servants, Wm Donkin, Henry Doeg, Chas Watson, John Letteney, Cuthbert Graham, John Bridon, John Eyons, Wm Cook, Richard Scott.

July-September

John Trewhitt, Geo. Collinson, Robt Wallis, Robt Briggs, John Fawdon, Joseph Edgar, Wm Marshall, Wm Rennoldson, Pere. Hutton, Wm Wilkinson & 3 servants, John Thackry & servant, Thos Taylor sen., Ed. Laing & son & servant, Francis Trewhitt & 3 servants, John Rennoldson & son & 3 servants, James White, Richard Shaw, John Gibson, Geo. Rennoldson, Robt Thompson, Ralph Hall, Andrew Hall, E. Curry, B. Barker, Geo. Smith & 3 servants, John Semple, John Ellison, Wm Pearson, Geo. Cram, Ed. Wilkinson, Chr. Henzell, Wm Ramshaw, Thos Allan, Wm Thobourn & servant, Geo. Maughlin, Joseph Moor, Thos Taylor jun., Wm Donkin, Henry Doeg, Chas Watson, John Letteney, Cuthbert Graham, John Bridon, Wm Cook, Richard Scott.

October-December

John Trewhitt, Robt Briggs, Wm Marshall, Wm Rennoldson, Pere. Hutton, Michael McTosh, Ed. Laing, Francis Trewhitt, Geo. Rennoldson, Robt Thompson, E. Curry, Geo. Smith & 4 servants, Wm Pearson, Geo. Cram, Wm Ostens, Wm Thobourn, Geo. Maughlin, Joseph Moor, T. E. Headlam & 3 servants, Wm Donkin, Henry Doeg, John Letteney, Cuthbert Graham, John Bridon, Wm Cook.

Fines levied on individual members

George Smith	Dr		Working St Luke Day 1753 self & 1 man	1	0
			do St Andrew Day 1753 2 men	1	0
As in former book fo. 342	7	6	Absent Easter Tuesday 1754	1	0
Absent Easter Tuesday 1753	1	0	Working St Paul Day 1754 & 2 men	1	6
Working St Paul's Day 1753 self & 2 men	1	6	Absent 24th June 1754	1	0
do St Mark's Day 1753 self & 8 men	4	6	Working May Day 1754 2 men	1	0
Absent 29th September 1753	1	0	Absent 30th September 1754 a quarter day	1	0
Working St James Day 1753 1 man		6	Working St Peter Day 1754 & 2 men	1	6
do St Matthew Day 1753 & 1 man	1	0	Absent Headmeeting Day 1754	1	0
Absent Head Meeting Day 1753	1	0	do Easter Tuesday 1755	1	0

Working St Paul self & 2 men	1	6
do 30th January self		6
Absent 24th June	1	0
Working St Mark 2 men	1	0
do May Day self & man	1	0
do Ascencion self & man	1	0
Working St Mark 1755 2 men	1	0
do St Philip & James self & man	1	0
do Ascencion Day self & man	1	0
Absent 29th December 1755	1	0
Working St James Day 3 men	1	6
Absent Michaelmas Monday	1	0
Paid	£2 1	6
Absent Easter Tuesday 1756	1	0
Working New Years Day self & six men	3	6
do Jan. 30th self & 4 men	2	6
do Candlemas Day self & 2 men	1	6
do St Matthias self & 4 men	2	6
do Lady Day self & 4 men	2	6
Absent 24 June	1	0
Working May Day self & 3 men	2	0
do 29th May and 2 men	1	6
do Whitsun Monday & 3 men	2	0
do Whitsun Tuesday self		6
do St Barnabas self		6
Absent 29th September	1	0
Working St John's self		6
do St Peter self & man	1	0
do St Bartholomew self & 2 men	1	6
Absent Michaelmas Monday	1	0
do Head Meeting Day	1	0
Working All Saints self & man	1	0
do St Andrew self & man	1	0

do St Thomas self & 3 men	2	0
Paid	£1 11	0
Absent 29 September 1757	1	0
Working St Peter self & 2 men	1	6
do St James self & 2 men	1	6
do St Bartholomew self & 2 men	1	6
do St Matthew self & 2 men	1	6
Absent Headmeeting day 1757	1	0
Working Michaelmas Day 2 men	1	0
do St Luke Day & 3 men	2	0
do St Simon & St Jude 3 men	1	6
do All Saints Day & 2 men	1	6
do 5 November 1757 3 men	1	6
do St Thomas Day 2 men	1	0
Paid	16	6
Absent Easter Tuesday 1758	1	0
Working St Paul Day & 2 men	1	6
do 30th January 3 men	1	6
do Candlemas Day & 2 men	1	6
do St Matthias Day 2 men	1	0
do Annunciation Day 2 men	1	0
Absent Midsummer Day	1	0
Working St Mark Day 3 men	1	6
do May Day 2 men	1	0
Absent 29th September	1	0
Working St Peter Day 3 men	1	6
do St James Day 2 men	1	0
do St Bartholomew Day 3 men	1	6

do St Matthew Day 2 men	1	0
Absent Head Meeting Day 1758	1	0
Working St Michael's Day 2 men	1	0
do St Simon & St Jude self & 2 men	1	6
do All Saints Day 2 men	1	0
do St Andrews Day 2 men	1	0
do St Thomas Day 2 men	1	0

Paid	£1	3	6

do New Years Day 1759 & 2 men	1	6
do 6 January & 2 men	1	6
do St Pauls Day 2 men	1	0
do 30 January 2 men	1	0
do Candlemas Day & 2 men	1	6
do St Matthias Day & 2 men	1	6
do Easter Monday 2 men	1	0
Absent Easter Tuesday	1	0
do 25th June	1	0
Working Easter Tuesday 2 men	1	0
do May Day 2 men	1	0
do St Barnabas Day 2 men	1	0
Absent 29th September	1	0
Working St Bartholomews Day 2 men	1	0
do St Matthias Day 2 men	1	0
Absent 27th December	1	0
Working St Michaels Day 2 men	1	0
do 5th November 2 men	1	0
do St Thomas Day 2 men	1	0
do St Paul Day 1760 2 men	1	0
do King Charles Martyrdom 2 men	1	0
do Candlemas Day 2 men	1	0
do Lady Day 2 men	1	0
Absent Easter Tuesday	1	0

Paid	£1	6	0

Absent 29th September	1	0
Working 24th June 2 men	1	0
do St James Day 2 men	1	0
Absent 27th December	1	0
Working St Lukes Day 2 men	1	0
do All Saints Day 2 men	1	0
do 5th November 2 men	1	0
Absent 24th March 1761	1	0
Working Epiphany 3 men	1	6
do 30th January 3 men	1	6
do Candlemas Day	1	6
Absent 24th June	1	0
Working Lady Day 3 men	1	6
do St Barnabas 2 men	1	0
Absent 29th September	1	0
Working St Peter Day 2 men	1	0
do St James Day 3 men	1	6
do St Bartholomew Day 2 men	1	0
do St Michael Day 2 men	1	0
do St Simon & Jude 2 men	1	0
do 5th November 2 men	1	0
do St Andrew 3 men	1	6
do St Thomas 2 men	1	0
Absent Head meeting day	1	0
do Easter Tuesday 1762	1	0
Working Epiphany 4 men	2	0
do St Paul 4 men	2	0
do King Charles Martyrdom 4 men	2	0
do Candlemas 4 men	2	0
do St Matthias 4 men	2	0
do Lady Day 3 men	1	6
do Easter Monday 4 men	2	0

Paid	£2	1	6

Absent 24th June	1	0
Working Easter Tuesday 3 men	1	6
do May Day 3 men	1	6
do Ascension Day 3 men	1	6
do 29th May 3 men	1	6
man		6
do Whitson Tuesday 1		
do St Barnabas 3 men	1	6

Absent 29th September	1	0
Working St John Baptist 3 men	1	6
do St Peter 3 men	1	6
do St Bartholomew 3 men	1	6
do St Matthew 3 men	1	6
Absent Easter Tuesday 1763	1	0
Working St John 2 men	1	0
do Epiphany 3 men	1	6
do St Paul 1 man		6
do Candlemas 1 man		6
do St Matthias 1 man		6
do Lady Day 1 man		6
Absent 29th September	1	0
Working St John Baptist 2 men	1	0
do St Peter 2 men	1	0
Paid	£1 4	6

Absent Head meeting day	1	0
Working St Michael 2 men	1	0
do St Luke 2 men	1	0
do St Simon & Jude 2 men	1	0
do All Saints do	1	0
do 5th November do	1	0
do St Andrew do	1	0
do St Thomas do	1	0
Paid	8	0

Absent Easter Tuesday 1764	1	0
Working St Paul 2 men	1	0
do King Charles do	1	0
do Candlemas do	1	0
do St Matthias 3 men	1	6
Absent Midsummer Day	1	0
Working St Mark Day 2 men	1	0
do May Day do	1	0
do 29th May do	1	0
do Ascension Day do	1	0
Absent 29th September	1	0
Working St Peter Day 2 men	1	0
do St James do	1	0

do St Bartholomew do	1	0
do St Matthew do	1	0
Paid	15	6
Absent Head Meeting Day	1	0
Working St Michael 2 men	1	0
do St Luke do	1	0
do All Saints do	1	0
do 5th November do	1	0
do St Andrew 3 men	1	6
do St Thomas do	1	6
do St Stephen 2 men	1	0
Absent Easter Tuesday 1765	1	0
Working Circumcision 2 men	1	0
do St Paul do	1	0
do King Charles M. do	1	0
do Lady Day do	1	0
Paid	14	0

Absent Midsummer Day	1	0
Working St Mark 2 men	1	0
do St Philip & James do	1	0
do Ascension Day do	1	0
do Whitsun Tuesday do	1	0
do 29th May do	1	0
do St Barnabas do	1	0
Absent 29th September	1	0
Working St John Baptist 2 men	1	0
do St Peter do	1	0
do St James do	1	0
do St Bartholomew do	1	0
do St Matthew do	1	0
Absent Head meeting day	1	0
Working St Luke 2 men	1	0
do St Simon & Jude do	1	0
do All Saints do	1	0
do St Andrew do	1	0
Paid	13	0
Carrd Fwd	5	0

Absent Easter Tuesday 1766	1	0
Working Epiphany 2 men	1	0
do St Paul do	1	0

do 30th January do	1	0
do St Matthias do	1	0
do Lady Day do	1	0
do Easter Tuesday do	1	0
Absent Midsummer Day	1	0
Working May Day 3 men	1	6
do St Barnabas do	1	6
Paid	16	0
Absent 29th September	1	0
Working St John Baptist 3 men	1	6
do St James do	1	6
Absent 27th December	1	0
Working St Michael 3 men	1	6
do St Luke do	1	6
do St Simon & Jude do	1	6
do All Saints do	1	6
do 5th November do	1	6
Absent 21st April 1767	1	0
Working Epiphany 3 men	1	6
do 30th January do	1	6
do Purification do	1	6
do Saint Matthias 4 men	2	0
Absent 24th June	1	0
Working Easter Tuesday 2 men	1	0
do St Mark 3 men	1	6
do St Philip & James do	1	6
do Asencion Day do	1	6
do 29th May do	1	6
do St Mark do	1	6
Absent 29th September	1	0
Working Michaelmas Day 2 men	1	0
do St Peter & Paul 3 men	1	6
do St James do	1	6
do St Bartholomew do	1	6
do St Matthew 2 men	1	0
Absent Head meeting day	1	0
Working St Michael 3 men	1	6
do St Simon & Jude do	1	6
do St Andrew do	1	6
Paid	£2 2	6
Absent Easter Tuesday 1768	1	0

One quarterly payment instead of holiday workings for himself	1	0
Three servants	1	6
Absent Midsummer Day	1	0
One quarterly payment himself	1	0
3 servants	1	6
Absent 29th September	1	0
One quarterly payment self & 3 servants	2	6
Absent Head meeting day	1	0
One quarterly payment	2	6
Absent Easter Tuesday 1769	1	0
One quarterly payment	2	6
Absent 24th June	1	0
Quarterly payment	2	6
Paid	15	0
Carrd Fwd	6	0
Absent 29th September	1	0
Quarterly payment	2	6
Absent Head Meeting Day	1	0
Quarterly payment self & 2 servants	2	0
Absent Easter Tuesday 1770	1	0
Quarterly payment	2	0
Absent Midsummer Day	1	0
Quarterly payment	2	0
Absent 29th September Deceased	1	0
Quarterly payment	2	0
Paid	£1 1	6
Absent Head Meeting Day	1	0
Quarterly payment	2	0
Absent Easter Tuesday 1771	1	0
Quarterly payment	2	0
Absent Midsummer Day	1	0
Quarterly payment	2	0
Absent Michaelmas Day	1	0
Quarterly payment	2	0
Absent Head Meeting Day	1	0
Quarterly payment	2	0
Absent Easter Tuesday	1	0
Quarterly payment	2	0
Absent Midsummer Day	1	0

Quarterly payment	2	0
Absent 29th September	1	0
Quarterly payment	2	0
Absent Head meeting day	1	0
Quarterly payment	2	0
Paid	£1 7	0
Absent Easter Tuesday 1773	1	0
Quarterly payment self & 1 servant	1	6
Absent Midsummer Day	1	0
Quarterly payment	1	6
Absent 29th September	1	0
Quarterly payment self & 2 servants	2	0
Absent Headmeeting day	1	0
Quarterly payment	2	0
Absent Easter Tuesday 1774	1	0
Quarterly payment	2	0
Absent Midsummer Day	1	0
Quarterly payment	2	0
Absent Michaelmas Day	1	0
Quarterly payment	2	0
Absent Head meeting day	1	0
Quarterly payment	2	0
Absent Easter Tuesday 1775	1	0
Quarterly payment	2	0
Absent Midsummer Day	1	0
Quarterly payment	2	0
Absent 29th September	1	0
Quarterly payment	2	0
Absent Head meeting day	1	0
Quarterly payment	2	0
Absent Easter Tuesday 1776	1	0
Quarterly payment	2	0
Absent 24 June & quarterly payment	3	0

Absent 30 September & quarterly money	3	0
do Headmeeting day do	3	0
do Easter Tuesday 1777 do	2	0
do 24th June do	2	0
do 29th September do	2	0
do 27th December do	2	0
do 22nd April 1778 do	2	0
do 24th June do	2	0
do 29th September do	2	0
do Head meeting day do	2	0
do 29th September do	2	0
do 27th December do	2	0
Paid	£3 7	0

Wm Lambert	Dr		
1778 Absent 24 June & quarterly money		2	0
do 5 October		1	0
1780 Absent 24 June & quarterly money		2	0
1783 Absent 29 September		1	0
Paid		6	0
1784 June 24 absent & quarterly money		2	0
1790 Oct. 4 short			6
1792 Apr. 15 absent & quarterly money		2	0
1801 April 7 absent		2	0
1803 June 24 absent & quarterly money		2	0
1805 Sept. 30 —do—		2	0
Paid		11	0
Deceased			

INDICES

INDEX OF PLACES

INDEX OF NAMES

311*—indicates that the entry in question occurs more than once on the
same page.
(—), Thomas, indicates that only the christian name appears.
Atkinson, (—), indicates that only the surname appears.
Anderson, (—), widow of, will be found in the text as Widd. Anderson.
Wilkinson, John widow of, will be found in the text as John Wilkinsons
widdow.
In the section listing Orders and Resolutions—the page number has been
quoted first with the item number in brackets i.e. 13(7).

335

GENERAL INDEX